# United Nations Conference on Trade and Development (UNCTAD)



This book is a much-needed new examination of the United Nations Conference on Trade and Development (UNCTAD), fully covering its history and current activities.

Ian Taylor and Karen Smith present a clear overview to an organization that is at times overlooked and seen to belong to a bygone era. All the key areas are covered by accessibly written chapters, including an overview of UNCTAD: what it is, why it was formed, and why it is important; how the organization operates today: what it does and how it does it; key criticisms made against the organization: is it relevant in today's world?; and emerging issues within the organization and its future direction.

In the current era of globalization and what appears to be the dominance of neoliberal economic thought, UNCTAD has sought to make itself germane to ongoing international debates. The implications of this for the organization's key remit, namely making the world a fairer place, are something that this book seeks to unpack.

The book will be of interest to all those interested in multilateralism, international trade issues and the global South.

**Ian Taylor** is Professor of International Relations in the School of International Relations, University of St. Andrews; Associate Professor Extraordinary, University of Stellenbosch, South Africa; and Visiting Lecturer, Mbarara University of Science and Technology, Uganda.

**Karen Smith** is Lecturer in the Department of Political Science at the University of Stellenbosch, South Africa.

## Routledge Global Institutions

Edited by Thomas G. Weiss
*The CUNY Graduate Center, New York, USA*
and Rorden Wilkinson
*University of Manchester, UK*

### About the Series

The Global Institutions Series is designed to provide readers with comprehensive, accessible, and informative guides to the history, structure, and activities of key international organizations. Every volume stands on its own as a thorough and insightful treatment of a particular topic, but the series as a whole contributes to a coherent and complementary portrait of the phenomenon of global institutions at the dawn of the millennium.

Books are written by recognized experts, conform to a similar structure, and cover a range of themes and debates common to the series. These areas of shared concern include the general purpose and rationale for organizations, developments over time, membership, structure, decision-making procedures, and key functions. Moreover, current debates are placed in historical perspective alongside informed analysis and critique. Each book also contains an annotated bibliography and guide to electronic information as well as any annexes appropriate to the subject matter at hand.

The volumes currently published or under contract include:

**The United Nations and Human Rights (2005)**
A guide for a new era
*by Julie Mertus (American University)*

**The UN Secretary General and Secretariat (2005)**
*by Leon Gordenker (Princeton University)*

**United Nations Global Conferences (2005)**
*by Michael G. Schechter (Michigan State University)*

**The UN General Assembly (2005)**
*by M.J. Peterson (University of Massachusetts, Amherst)*

**Internal Displacement (2006)**
Conceptualization and its consequences
*by Thomas G. Weiss (The CUNY Graduate Center) and David A. Korn*

**Global Environmental Institutions (2006)**
*by Elizabeth R. DeSombre (Wellesley College)*

**The UN Security Council (2006)**
Practice and promise
*by Edward C. Luck (Columbia University)*

**The World Intellectual Property Organization (2006)**
Resurgence and the development agenda
*by Chris May (University of Lancaster)*

**The North Atlantic Treaty Organization (2007)**
The enduring alliance
*by Julian Lindley-French (European Union Centre for Security Studies)*

**The International Monetary Fund (2007)**
Politics of conditional lending
*by James Raymond Vreeland (Yale University)*

**The Group of 7/8 (2007)**
*by Hugo Dobson (University of Sheffield)*

**The World Economic Forum (2007)**
A multi-stakeholder approach to global governance
*by Geoffrey Allen Pigman (Bennington College)*

**The International Committee of the Red Cross (2007)**
A neutral humanitarian actor
*by David Forsythe (University of Nebraska) and Barbara Ann Rieffer-Flanagan (Central Washington University)*

**The Organization for Security and Co-operation in Europe (2007)**
*by David J. Galbreath (University of Aberdeen)*

**United Nations Conference on Trade and Development (UNCTAD) (2007)**
*by Ian Taylor (University of St. Andrews) and Karen Smith (University of Stellenbosch)*

**A Crisis of Global Institutions? (2007)**
Multilateralism and international security
*by Edward Newman (United Nations University)*

**The World Trade Organization (2007)**
Law, economics, and politics
*by Bernard Hoekman (World Bank) and Petros Mavroidis (Columbia University)*

**The African Union**
Challenges of globalization, security and governance
*by Samuel M. Makinda (Murdoch University) and Wafula Okumu (McMaster University)*

**The World Bank**
From reconstruction to development to equity
*by Katherine Marshall (Georgetown University)*

**Organisation for Economic Co-operation and Development**
*by Richard Woodward (University of Hull)*

**Non-Governmental Organizations in Global Politics**
*by Peter Willetts (City University, London)*

**Multilateralism in the South**
An analysis
*by Jacqueline Anne Braveboy-Wagner (City College of New York)*

**The International Labour Organization**
*by Steve Hughes (University of Newcastle)*

**The Commonwealth(s) and Global Governance**
*by Timothy Shaw (Royal Roads University)*

**UNHCR**
The politics and practice of refugee protection into the twenty-first century
*by Gil Loescher (University of Oxford), James Milner (University of Oxford), and Alexander Betts (University of Oxford)*

**The International Organization for Standardization and the Global Economy**
Setting standards
*by Craig Murphy (Wellesley College) and JoAnne Yates (Massachusetts Institute of Technology)*

**The International Olympic Committee**
*by Jean-Loup Chappelet (IDHEAP Swiss Graduate School of Public Administration) and Brenda Kübler-Mabbott*

**The European Union**
*by Clive Archer (Manchester Metropolitan University)*

**The World Health Organization**
*by Kelley Lee (London School of Hygiene and Tropical Medicine)*

**Internet Governance**
The new frontier of global institutions
*by John Mathiason (Syracuse University)*

**Shaping the Humanitarian World**
*by Peter Walker (Tufts University)*

**Contemporary Human Rights Ideas**
*by Bertrand G. Ramcharan (Geneva Graduate Institute of International Studies)*

**For further information regarding the series, please contact:**

Craig Fowlie, Publisher, Politics & International Studies
Taylor & Francis
2 Park Square, Milton Park, Abingdon
Oxford OX14 4RN, UK

+44 (0)207 842 2057 Tel
+44 (0)207 842 2302 Fax

Craig.Fowlie@tandf.co.uk
www.routledge.com

# United Nations Conference on Trade and Development (UNCTAD)

Ian Taylor and Karen Smith

Routledge
Taylor & Francis Group
LONDON AND NEW YORK

First published 2007
by Routledge
2 Park Square, Milton Park, Abingdon, Oxon OX14 4RN

Simultaneously published in the USA and Canada
by Routledge
711 Third Avenue, New York, NY 10017

*Routledge is an imprint of the Taylor & Francis Group, an informa business*



Typeset in Times New Roman by
Taylor & Francis Books



*British Library Cataloguing in Publication Data*
A catalogue record for this book is available from the British Library

*Library of Congress Cataloging in Publication Data*
A catalog record for this book has been requested

ISBN 978–0–415–37020–2 (hbk)
ISBN 978–0–415–37019–6 (pbk)
ISBN 978–0–203–02977–0 (ebk)

# Contents

# Foreword

The current volume is the fifteenth in a dynamic series on "global institutions." The series strives (and, based on the volumes published to date, succeeds) to provide readers with definitive guides to the most visible aspects of what we know as "global governance." Remarkable as it may seem, there exist relatively few books that offer in-depth treatments of prominent global bodies and processes, much less an entire series of concise and complementary volumes. Those that do exist are either out of date, inaccessible to the non-specialist reader, or seek to develop a specialized understanding of particular aspects of an institution or process rather than offer an overall account of its functioning. Similarly, existing books have often been written in highly technical language or have been crafted "in-house" and are notoriously self-serving and narrow.

The advent of electronic media has helped by making information, documents, and resolutions of international organizations more widely available, but it has also complicated matters. The growing reliance on the Internet and other electronic methods of finding information about key international organizations and processes has served, ironically, to limit the educational materials to which most readers have ready access—namely, books. Public relations documents, raw data, and loosely refereed web sites do not make for intelligent analysis. Official publications compete with a vast amount of electronically available information, much of which is suspect because of its ideological or self-promoting slant. Paradoxically, a growing range of purportedly independent web sites offering analyses of the activities of particular organizations has emerged, but one inadvertent consequence has been to frustrate access to basic, authoritative, critical, and well-researched texts. The market for such has actually been reduced by the ready availability of varying quality electronic materials.

For those of us who teach, research, and practice in the area, this access to information has been particulary frustrating. We were delighted, then, when Routledge saw the value of a series that bucks this trend and provides key reference points to the most significant global institutions. They are betting that serious students and professionals will want serious analyses. We have assembled a first-rate line-up of authors to address that market. Our intention, then, is to provide one-stop shopping for all readers—students (both undergraduate and postgraduate), interested negotiators, diplomats, practitioners from nongovernmental and intergovernmental organizations, and interested parties alike—seeking information about the most prominent institutional aspects of global governance.

## The United Nations Conference on Trade and Development

UNCTAD is something of an anomaly among global institutions. Only ever given the status of a permanent forum (or "conference") for intergovernmental deliberation with attendant research, policy analysis, and data collection facilities rather than a formal organization, it has nevertheless long encapsulated the hopes and desires of many developing countries for a "new international economic order"—something of an invective after the collapse of North-South dialogue in the mid-1970s.

Conceived as a natural gathering spot for Third World leaders that built upon growing solidarity following the mass rounds of decolonization in the wake of World War II, UNCTAD sought, beginning in 1964, to give form to ideas that challenged the way in which the global economy had been organized as well as those institutions that enabled former colonial powers to maintain and extend their economic (and political) relationships with the newly independent countries. UNCTAD's primary goal was to put in place an alternative system of international trade. Instead of liberalized markets with disproportionate benefits for the industrial North, and of protection for such markets (precisely those to which developing countries required access), UNCTAD sought to change the ground rules for the General Agreement on Tariffs and Trade[1] and to bring about substantive and independent (rather than reflective)[2] development among developing countries and especially the poorest among them. In short, it sought to alter the fact that "the rich get richer and the poor get poorer"—in international trade and development as elsewhere.

UNCTAD had more success in flagging issues and changing vocabulary than in negotiating change in such issues as commodities and trade preferences. Its meetings on both specific (for instance, specific commodities, insurance, trade with socialist countries, and shipping) and general topics (for instance, the terms of trade, generalized preferences, international development assistance, investment, and transnational corporations) led to a discussion in the United Nations General Assembly of the much trumpeted (but ultimately unrealized) 1974 call for the creation of a New International Economic Order (NIEO).

UNCTAD's more recent history has been one of compromise peppered with scant progress and diminished visibility. The radical ideas that once underpinned UNCTAD have since given way to a slightly modified version of liberal orthodoxy, and it has successfully fought off calls to disband it. UNCTAD nevertheless retains an important role as critic, forum, and source of technical expertise. It has, among other things, been widely praised for its technical assistance in assisting countries with the notoriously thorny process of acceding to the World Trade Organization (WTO).[3] UNCTAD's story, then, is one of hope unrealized. But this headline belies the very real and worthwhile work that has come out of the institution since it was created. The institution provides a fascinating lens into the evolution of international politics and economics over the last four decades.

Clearly we needed a book that scratched beneath the surface of this fascinating institution for our series. As both of us have written about this institution and one of us worked in the Secretariat for a decade,[4] we chose with care the contributors to this volume. We were delighted, then, when Ian Taylor, Senior Lecturer in International Relations at the University of St. Andrews, UK and Professor Extraordinary in Political Science at the University of Stellenbosch, South Africa, accepted our invitation to write this book for us. Ian has made his career traversing the political economy of development in the global South, a topic on which he speaks and writes authoritatively. He is the author of, among other recent volumes, *China and Africa: Engagement and Compromise*; *NEPAD: Towards Africa's Development or Another False Start*; and *Stuck in Middle Gear: South Africa's Post-Apartheid Foreign Relations.*[5] Joining forces with him is Karen Smith, Lecturer in International Relations at the University of Stellenbosch. Karen is the Secretary-General of the United Nations Association of South Africa (UNA-SA) and lectures on International Organizations.

As we are sure you will agree, this is an excellent book on an important global institution. It deserves to be read by all interested in development, governance, and the global economy. As always, comments and suggestions from readers are welcome.

Thomas G. Weiss, The CUNY Graduate Center, New York, USA
Rorden Wilkinson, University of Manchester, UK
December 2006

# Acknowledgments

This study has benefited from the advice and help of Shigehisa Kasahara of UNCTAD in Geneva, who freely answered questions about various facets of UNCTAD's work and who provided access to his own unpublished work on the organization. We are truly grateful for his help.

We would also like to thank the librarians at the University of St. Andrews and the University of Stellenbosch for their help and assistance in obtaining various materials on UNCTAD.

All errors and omissions remain our own.

# Abbreviations

| | |
|---|---|
| APEC | Asia Pacific Economic Cooperation |
| ASEAN | Association of Southeast Asian Nations |
| ASEM | Asia Europe Meeting |
| BWIs | Bretton Woods Institutions |
| CICT | Commission on International Commodity Trade |
| DAC | Development Assistance Committee |
| DFA | Department of Foreign Affairs (South Africa) |
| DITE | Division on Investment, Technology, and Enterprise Development |
| ECLAC | United Nations Economic Commission for Latin America and the Caribbean |
| ECOSOC | United Nations Economic and Social Council |
| EEC | European Economic Community |
| FAO | Food and Agriculture Organization |
| G-8 | Group of Eight |
| G-20 | Group of 20 |
| G-77 | Group of Seventy-Seven |
| GATS | General Agreement on Trade in Services |
| GATT | General Agreement on Tariffs and Trade |
| GDP | Gross Domestic Product |
| GNP | Gross National Product |
| GSP | Generalized System of Preferences |
| IBRD | International Bank for Reconstruction and Development |
| ICAs | International Commodity Agreements |
| ICCICA | Interim Coordinating Committee on International Commodity Agreements |
| IFIs | International Financial Institutions |
| IMF | International Monetary Fund |
| IPC | Integrated Program for Commodities |

| | |
|---|---|
| ITO | International Trade Organization |
| LDCs | Least Developed Countries |
| MDGs | Millennium Development Goals |
| MFA | Multi-Fiber Arrangement |
| MFN | Most Favored Nation |
| NAFTA | North American Free Trade Agreement |
| NAM | Non-Aligned Movement |
| NEPAD | New Economic Partnership for Africa's Development |
| NGO | Non-Governmental Organization |
| NIEO | New International Economic Order |
| OECD | Organization for Economic Cooperation and Development |
| OPEC | Organization of Petroleum Exporting Countries |
| SAPs | Structural Adjustment Programs |
| TDR | Trade and Development Report |
| TNCs | Transnational Corporations |
| TRIMS | Trade Related Investment Measures |
| TRIPS | Trade Related Intellectual Property Rights |
| UN | United Nations |
| UNCTAD | United Nations Conference on Trade and Development |
| UNDP | United Nations Development Programme |
| UNESCO | United Nations Educational, Scientific and Cultural Organization |
| UNGA | United Nations General Assembly |
| WHO | World Health Organization |
| WTO | World Trade Organization |

# Introduction

The United Nations Conference on Trade and Development (UNCTAD) was formed in 1964 to "create a forum in which the more prosperous member countries [of the United Nations] would come under pressure to agree to measures benefiting the less-developed countries."[1] More specifically, its formation was "a deliberate effort to use international bureaucracy and conference diplomacy to alter current norms affecting trade and development,"[2] and the organization has been termed the "intervener between poor and rich states."[3] As will be explained later, though originally a one-off conference, UNCTAD evolved into a permanent organization as an appendage of the United Nations General Assembly (UNGA). However, as an appendage, it is not a dedicated agency with an autonomous budget, nor does it have a supreme governing body. This is deliberate as it protects UNCTAD from having its budget reduced or even the organization being shut down. UNCTAD's annual operational budget is approximately $55 million, which is drawn from the United Nations (UN) regular budget and is approved by the UNGA. In addition, technical cooperation activities, financed from extra-budgetary sources, are around $24 million a year, financed by a mixture of trust funds, funds from the UNDP, and the Development Account of the United Nations program budget.

UNCTAD has traditionally been the one UN agency which is regarded as *the* multilateral site where the global South might articulate its needs and problems and where international development is firmly on the agenda—as opposed to other multilateral institutions, which are perceived by many to be overly dominated by the developed world. The Final Act of the founding Conference in 1964 has set the tone for the organization, with its mandate being "to seek a better and more effective system of international economic cooperation … and lay the foundations of a better world economic order."[4] The success or otherwise of the organization in achieving its mandate will be discussed in this book. A key criticism of the organization is that it has been sabotaged by the North and prevented from making key pronouncements—indeed UNCTAD's alternative meaning has been derisorily labeled "Under No Conditions Take a Decision." But before getting to that, at this stage it is important to lay out UNCTAD's fundamental functions. These are, namely, to advance global trade; to frame principles and policies on this trade; to evaluate and smooth the progress of co-ordinating the various roles and activities of other UN institutions vis-à-vis international trade; to instigate acts and policies aimed at facilitating trade—again, in cooperation with UN bodies; and to be a site where governments and regional organizations might harmonize their commercial, trade and development policies. What this all means in practice is that UNCTAD is a multifaceted organization, which conducts research and investigations into trade-related issues, which promotes cooperation along these lines and which, finally, through its various conferences and meeting points, seeks to promote agreements as to how best to promote trade and development. The organization's membership currently stands at 192 countries, as found in Box 1.1.

### *Box 1.1* Members of UNCTAD

The following 192 countries are members of UNCTAD. The members of the Trade and Development Board are marked with an "*":

Afghanistan*
Albania*
Algeria*
Andorra
Angola*
Antigua
Argentina*
Armenia*
Australia*
Austria*
Azerbaijan*
Bahamas
Bahrain*
Bangladesh*
Barbados*
Belarus*
Belgium*
Belize
Benin*
Bhutan*
Bolivia*
Bosnia and Herzegovina
Botswana*
Brazil*
Brunei Darussalam
Bulgaria*
Burkina Faso*
Burundi*
Cambodia
Cameroon*
Canada*
Cape Verde
Central African Republic*
Chad*
Chile*
China*
Colombia*
Comoros
Congo*
Costa Rica*
Côte d'Ivoire*
Croatia*
Cuba*

Cyprus*
Czech Republic*
North*
DR Congo*
Denmark*
Djibouti
Dominica*
Dominican Republic*
Ecuador*
Egypt*
El Salvador*
Equatorial Guinea*
Eritrea
Estonia
Ethiopia*
Fiji
Finland*
France*
FYR of Macedonia*
Gabon*
Gambia
Georgia*
Germany*
Ghana*
Greece*
Grenada*
Guatemala*
Guinea*
Guinea-Bissau
Guyana*
Haiti*
Holy See
Honduras*
Hungary*
Iceland*
India*
Indonesia*
Iran*
Iraq*
Ireland*
Israel*
Italy*
Jamaica*
Japan*
Jordan*
Kazakhstan
Kenya*
Kiribati
Kuwait*
Kyrgyzstan
Laos
Latvia*
Lebanon*
Lesotho*
Liberia*
Libya*
Liechtenstein*
Lithuania*
Luxembourg*
Madagascar*
Malawi
Malaysia*
Maldives
Mali*
Malta *
Marshall Islands
Mauritania*
Mauritius*
Mexico*
Micronesia
Monaco
Mongolia*
Morocco*
Mozambique*
Myanmar*
Namibia*
Nauru
Nepal*
Netherlands*
New Zealand*
Nicaragua *
Niger
Nigeria*
Norway*
Oman*
Pakistan*
Palau
Panama*
Papua New Guinea*
Paraguay*
Peru*
Philippines*
Poland*
Portugal*
Qatar*
South Korea*
Moldova*
Romania *
Russian Federation*
Rwanda
St. Kitts and Nevis
St. Lucia
St. Vincent and the Grenadines
Samoa
San Marino
São Tomé and Príncipe*
Saudi Arabia*
Senegal*
Serbia and Montenegro*
Seychelles
Sierra Leone *
Singapore*
Slovakia*
Slovenia*
Solomon Islands
Somalia*
South Africa*

| | | |
|---|---|---|
| Spain* | Timor Leste | United Kingdom* |
| Sri Lanka* | Togo* | United States of America* |
| Sudan * | Tonga | Uruguay * |
| Suriname* | Trinidad and Tobago* | Uzbekistan |
| Swaziland | Tunisia* | Vanuatu |
| Sweden * | Turkey * | Venezuela* |
| Switzerland* | Turkmenistan | Viet Nam * |
| Syria* | Tuvalu | Yemen* |
| Tajikistan | Uganda* | Zambia* |
| Tanzania* | Ukraine* | Zimbabwe* |
| Thailand * | United Arab Emirates* | |

Since its inception, and despite a mass of controversies around its very existence, UNCTAD has achieved some important international agreements. In trade, most notable of these is the Generalized System of Preference (GSP) of 1971.[5] The GSP has allowed developing countries to gain billions of dollars via the preferential treatment afforded their exports in the markets of the North. The Set of Multilaterally Agreed Equitable Principles and Rules for the Control of Restrictive Business Practices, agreed to in 1980 is also a trade-related agreement that UNCTAD can take credit for. In goods, international commodity agreements for a variety of commodities such as cocoa, sugar, natural rubber, tropical timber, tin, olive oil and wheat have been negotiated by UNCTAD, whilst the Common Fund for Commodities, established to make available financial support for the operation of international stocks and for research and development in the field of commodities was arrived at in 1989. UNCTAD has also led the way in marshalling support for the least developed countries (LDCs), through such measures as the Special New Program of Action for the LDCs of 1981, the Program of Action for the LDCs for the 1990s of 1990 and the Agreement on a Global Framework for Transit Transport Cooperation between Landlocked and Transit Developing Countries and the Donor Countries of 1995. UNCTAD can also claim part of the credit for agreements on aid targets, such as the 0.7 percent of GNP target for donor countries.

The structure of the book proceeds as follows. Chapter 1 provides the basic historical background to the organization. It begins with a prelude of the rapid decolonization efforts of the 1950s and early 1960s, which leads up to the story of UNCTAD's two-year preparatory period and founding in 1964. The "golden years" and the organization's period of identity crises brings us to the uncertainty of the twenty-first century. Before discussing the detailed history of UNCTAD, two chapters on the organizational structure of the body and its output and productivity are described and analyzed.

Chapter 2 discusses the Secretariat structure, examining in detail how UNCTAD functions and what its Secretariat in Geneva performs. The UNCTAD Secretariat provides substantive and technical services to the intergovernmental bodies of UNCTAD in their discussions and deliberations. It undertakes research, policy analysis and data collection to provide substantive inputs for the discussions of the experts and government representatives in these intergovernmental bodies. It also provides a series of technical assistance programs and projects in support of developing countries, paying particular attention to the special handicaps of the least developed countries. The current secretary-general of UNCTAD, Dr Supachai Panitchpakdi, heads a Secretariat made up of about 400 staff members with an annual operating budget of approximately $50 million, with $25 million of extra budgetary technical assistance funds.

Chapter 3 then examines the research and analysis aspect of UNCTAD's work. The *Trade and Development Report,* which analyzes economic trends and policy issues of international concern, is perhaps the best-known UNCTAD publication, but the organization produces a whole host of research that is increasingly relied upon by developing nations for information. In the current WTO-dominated milieu, the research activities of UNCTAD have been identified as a key comparative advantage of the organization, and something which UNCTAD has developed as a major output.

Returning to the history of the organization, Chapters 4 and 5 discuss the historical trajectory and development of UNCTAD as a multilateral body, tracing its origins to today, looking at how UNCTAD played a major role in the NIEO moment of the 1970s, as well as the gradual retreat and arguably, eclipse, during the 1980s, these chapters provide a thorough examination of UNCTAD's various policy positions and how these relate to the broader context of the global political economy and, in particular, the rise to prominence of neoliberalism. Chapter 6 follows on from these two chapters with a discussion of how and where UNCTAD fits in with regard to the WTO. Given that the WTO performs many of the duties that UNCTAD once aspired to or at least sought to influence, the future position of UNCTAD and its relationship to the WTO is of fundamental importance, and is discussed in this chapter. Finally, Chapter 7 provides a conclusion and pointers to the future of UNCTAD and where it might consider targeting its energies in the coming years.

# 1 Historical background

UNCTAD's founding reflected the growth in membership of newly independent states within the United Nations (UN). A large number of the elites of these new entities keenly felt the iniquity of the world order upon which they had been launched. UNCTAD and the later call for a "New International Economic Order" (NIEO) therefore was a rejoinder to problems encountered by developing countries as a result of the creation and operation of the Bretton Woods Institutions (BWIs).[1] The history of UNCTAD stakes out the rise of these positions in global diplomacy and equally, their effective demise.

Indeed, the very *raison d'etre* of UNCTAD sprang from developments after World War II, when the BWIs were established as a means to avoid crises of the type that had characterized the 1930s and, it was believed, had led to World War II. The key principle behind the BWIs was to promote "free trade" and dismantle trade barriers and restrictions on commerce, while promoting the global "free market." For the most part, issues regarding international trade were addressed within the BWIs—particularly the General Agreement on Tariffs and Trade (GATT)—on the principle of "most favored nation" (MFN), with a strong emphasis on the ideas of give-and-take and reciprocity, as well as non-discrimination against fellow members. GATT itself was initially signed in 1947 and was intended to make available an international forum to encourage "free trade" between member states by regulating and reducing tariffs on products that were traded, as well as developing an instrument for settling trade disputes.

In 1948, the Havana Charter established an International Trade Organization (ITO) to regulate global trade and to oversee issues pertaining to commodities. Latin American countries, many of which formed the core of the original GATT, had been promoting the establishment of a multilateral trading regime to advance their own economies. However, the United States never ratified the Havana Charter and as a consequence, the ITO failed to gain the requisite number of signatories and thus did not come into existence. In contrast to the planned ITO, the GATT did not include terms regarding commodity accords or foreign investment rules or preferential trading systems for the developing world. Issues pertaining to trade in commodities (originally a remit of the ITO) were actually assumed by the United Nations Economic and Social Council (ECOSOC). At the same time, the Interim Coordinating Committee on International Commodity Agreements (ICCICA) was established to manage action on international commodity issues. Later, in 1954, the Commission on International Commodity Trade (CICT) was created within the ICCICA to examine ways to stabilize commodity prices and their production for the global market. Meanwhile, multilateral developmental assistance was mainly supervised by the World Bank, while the Development Assistance Committee (DAC) of the Organization for Economic Cooperation and Development (OECD) handled bilateral aid. Issues pertaining to monetary collaboration at the international level were largely confined to the remit of the International Monetary Fund (IMF). In other words, global trade and development governance were fairly well covered by an array of organizations and institutions.

Yet, all these institutions worked within a milieu where the number of newly independent, post-colonial states—with all their attendant developmental issues and, in the case of many, dependence on commodities—was growing and where the coherence (and relevance) of this plethora of institutions was deemed problematic. Indeed, the newly emergent states quickly realized that all of these separate multilateral bodies were highly relevant to their future development, yet remained institutionally disconnected. The need for a coherent body to bring together the various issues handled separately by the above organizations was deemed more and more important by the new countries within the UN. Furthermore, the GATT system and its process of trade negotiations was seen by many to reproduce the power asymmetries in global commerce, with GATT talks invariably being conducted between the main producers and consumers for each separate product. Such a situation meant that the bargaining power of the producers (i.e. the developing world) was greatly lessened as in the main developing countries seldom made up the chief market shares as producers. As a result, power within the negotiating structures of the GATT was invariably in the hands of the developed world and was viewed by the new nations, as well as the Latin Americans, as inimical to their development.

Initially, the concerns of the developing world were expressed at and through the Asian-African Conference, convened in Bandung, Indonesia, 18–24 April 1955. The Asian-African Conference was a seminal event in the history of the post-colonial world for it was at Bandung that African and Asian nations first made tentative links within a political setting. Bandung itself had sprung from a concept that had first been suggested at a meeting of the Prime Ministers of Burma, Ceylon, India, Indonesia and Pakistan in Colombo, Ceylon in April 1953. This was formalized by the so-called "Colombo Powers" on 29 December 1954. Twenty-nine countries attended Bandung, a nascent bloc of developing world nations, and for many writers, the Asian-African Conference was of great and lasting importance in setting up the conditions for greater unity among the developing world.[2]

Bandung has since been described as "in essence a celebration of the wave of independence that had swept across Asia and was then cresting in Africa."[3] The motives for convening such a conference varied widely among the elites attending, as did their economic and political orientations. Nonetheless, Bandung did adopt a number of resolutions that have been described as "an augur of a future protest against the subordinating stays of the developing countries in the international system," and which established a set of normative values which aimed at a more equitable world order.[4] Interestingly, the GATT began to be aware of the issues being raised at Bandung. In 1958, the so-called "Haberler Report," in honor of Professor Gottfried Haberler, the chair of the panel of economists mandated by the GATT to examine why less-developed countries were failing to develop as rapidly as industrial nations, was published. The report, officially titled *Trends in International Trade,* offered guidelines for the GATT, and a number of changes, including a Declaration on the Promotion of Trade of Less-Developed Countries, were later adopted.

Bandung was followed by the Belgrade Conference of 1961 where the Non-Aligned Movement (NAM) was officially launched. At Belgrade a declaration containing the common views of delegates on international problems was issued that was in line with the general Bandung position, and an agreement on the summits of NAM being triennial was reached. The NAM was established as a loose multilateralist project with very little formal organization and this resulted in conference diplomacy becoming a specific characteristic and feature of non-alignment.[5] By confirming the "Spirit of Bandung" in 1961, the NAM also adopted a posture that rejected the bilateralist impulses that dominated the world through the system of Cold War alliances. Indeed, the "Bandung Era" lasted until approximately the formation of UNCTAD and was, during this period, the flag-carrier for the concerns and aspirations—as well as the flexing of muscles—of the newly post-colonial state elites.

This became more and more apparent as Africa and Asia emerged from colonialism. Indeed, in 1960, nearly 20 African states achieved independence. This massively augmented the ranks of those countries that had identified themselves with the Bandung message and swung the balance of numbers within the UN General Assembly (UNGA) in the favor of the developing world. Thus, as the 1960s progressed and the number of independent nations in the "Third World" grew, rising attention had to be paid to the problems being encountered by a growing number of UN members, problems that Bandung had highlighted and which the increased presence of new nations increasingly vocalized. As a consequence, the demands of the developing world began to take up more time and attention of the various bodies within the UN system. This was further stimulated by material conditions within the South as conditions for commodity prices became unstable in the 1960s. A demand for action by the UN on behalf of the new nations thus became ever more urgent.[6]

Equally, the BWIs were condemned for their oversight regarding the issues facing the new states and also because the status and standing of the socialist states of Eastern Europe was generally neglected. In short, the BWIs were in a weak position to safeguard the developmental aspirations of a growing portion of the world. And the fragmented nature of existing institutions for global governance stimulated a growing coalition within the newly independent nations for something to be done vis-à-vis the setting up of a unified body to consider their particular problems and prospects.

The above broad environment saw, in 1962, the Conference on Problems of Developing Countries, held in Cairo and attended by 36 country delegations. This Cairo meeting appealed for an international conference on "all vital questions relating to international trade, primary commodity trade and economic relations between developing and developed countries," the discussion of which was to take place within the UN.[7] The socialist states of Eastern Europe threw their weight behind this call and as a consequence ECOSOC made two crucial resolutions—917(XXXIV) and 963(XXXV), which requested such a meeting. Later, a resolution within the UN General Assembly, Resolution 1785(XVII), also demanded a conference on trade and development, and established a preparatory committee for this. This determination can be seen as a diplomatic victory for the developing countries, against the broad resistance of the developed states who eventually gave up their opposition to such calls for two key reasons. First, a Soviet threat to create an international trade organization convinced the West that it would be a strategic error to allow the developing world to set up such a body—sponsored by and with the active involvement of the Warsaw Pact countries—with no input or presence of the capitalist countries of the developed world. Second, and perhaps more importantly, the increasing majority of the developing countries in the UN left them with very few choices.[8] This then was the basic background to the establishment of UNCTAD, an event that was to take place two years after the Cairo Declaration.

## The formation

The 1964 Conference (known as UNCTAD I) was held in Geneva, Switzerland from 23 March to 16 June 1964. Representatives of 120 countries took part, along with a variety of international organizations. The main negotiations were clustered into six agenda items:

1 expansion of international trade and its significance for economic development;
2 global commodity problems;
3 trade in manufactured and semi-manufactured products;
4 improvement of the "invisible trade" of developing nations;
5 the development of regional economic groupings;
6 tnstitutional activities and methods to put into practice measures regarding the growth of international trade.

These agenda items were separated into five committees, whose conclusions were reported back to the Conference.

The Conference adopted the Final Act, setting out the principles upon which UNCTAD was to be based, which contained 15 General and 13 Special Principles to govern trade relations and policies (see p. 12). The underpinnings of these Principles were grounded in Raúl Prebisch's work.[9] Of note, the Principles were adopted by roll call and a number of developed countries voted against some or many of the Principles (others abstained). Those most systematically opposed to the Principles included Australia, Canada, the United Kingdom and the United States, while other developed nations also voted against specific Principles.

Overall, the Final Act grounded the future organization in promoting increased market access for exports from the developing world by using preferential access and dismantling protectionism for agricultural products in the developed world; regulating and steadying the international market for primary commodities, in order to counterbalance the diminishing terms of trade for the developing countries; and approving policies to boost financial flows to the post-colonial world.

The hand of Raúl Prebisch, the first secretary-general of UNCTAD, was very much in evidence in these Principles. In his report to the first plenary session of UNCTAD I in 1964, Prebisch had stated that the GATT had not been "efficacious" for the developing countries because it "is based upon the classic concept that the free play of international economic forces by itself leads to the optimum expansion of trade and the most efficient utilization of the world's productive resources."[10] Consequently, "the international community [i.e., the Western, capitalist economies] should recognize that it has a clear responsibility towards developing countries that have suffered deterioration in terms of trade in the same way as governments recognize a similar responsibility toward their domestic primary producers."[11]

Prebisch grounded his argument on the disparities between the nature of the demand for primary commodities and manufactured goods, i.e. low price and fluctuating incomes from the former. Prebisch argued that the prices that could be commanded for primary goods were so lacking in elasticity that relatively, it did not matter what producers did vis-à-vis increased efficiency, productivity or other means, increases in quantities exported would not result in greater receipts to the producers. This was compounded by the growth in technological innovation in the developed world, which meant that primary products and commodity-based economies were progressively being replaced by man-made products. Thus the demand and hence price for commodities was in perpetual decline. Prebisch warned that this would get worse for the developing world as time progressed and technology improved and that this meant that the gap between rich and poor in global terms would become more, not less. The message from Prebisch was that unless there were greater flows of developmental assistance, coupled with comprehensive commodity deals and implementation of compensatory financing systems (as a way of transferring income), the newly independent nations would be trapped at the bottom of the global division of labor in perpetuity. Simply dismantling barriers to trade, as per the GATT's remit, would not be sufficient to reverse this process. *Preferential* access of processed goods from the developing world to the North was what was needed, with tariff preferences in the North assisting, as well as aid.[12] This was not charity, but "compensation, a rebate to the Third World for the years of declining commodity purchasing power."[13]

Predictably, such rhetoric attracted a great deal of opposition from the developed world, who sought to block such positions being advanced. However, the majority of developing countries at UNCTAD I passed a set of resolutions that established the aforementioned Principles. The key Principles are summarized below and are important to note for their assertion of equality, sovereignty and the placing of development onto the central agenda of the international community:

*General Principle One* Economic relations between countries shall be based on respect for the principle of sovereign equality of all states, self-determination and non-interference in domestic affairs.

*General Principle Three* Every country has the sovereign right freely to trade with other countries, and freely to dispose of its natural resources in the interest of the economic development and well-being of its own people.

*General Principle Four* Economic development and social progress should be the common concern of the whole international community.

*General Principle Five* Developed countries should assist developing countries to speed up their economic and social progress and should encourage appropriate adjustments in their own economies to this end.

*General Principle Fifteen* The adoption of international policies and measures for the economic development of the developing countries shall take into account the individual characteristics and different stages of development of the developing countries, special attention being paid to the less developed among them, as an effective means of ensuring sustained growth with equitable opportunity for each developing country.

The Principles above set out UNCTAD's basic position. Following on from this, a decision was made at Geneva to convert UNCTAD into a *permanent* international institution and not just a one-off conference (as indeed the actual name of the organization, even today, implies). At Geneva there was a discussion over what type of body UNCTAD should become—whether it should be an organ of the UNGA (the developing world's position) or whether it should be under the ambit of ECOSOC (the developed world's favored solution). The developing world's opinion eventually triumphed, with the argument being that ECOSOC membership was inadequate and that not only did it not represent the developing world but also that its past energies in resolving concerns and issues of the developing world had been lackluster and wholly unproductive. The developing world in particular was keen to gain the backing and legitimization that only being an organ of the General Assembly could grant the new forum.[14]

Indeed, what came out of Geneva was a vision that saw UNCTAD being the main site where debate and discussion over policy regarding international trade and development issues might be thrashed out as a means by which consensus over such issues might be reached—and all backed by the UNGA.

## The early years

As a permanent organization, UNCTAD was established as a formal organ of the UNGA on 30 December 1964 by the General Assembly through Resolution 1995(XIX). In this resolution, the mandate and the structure of UNCTAD were established. As part of this structure, Article Two of the resolution stated that the conference would be called together "at intervals of not more than three years." The highest decision-making body of UNCTAD is the ministerial conference, at which member states make evaluations of current trade and development issues, confer regarding policy choices and put together global policy responses. The conference also sets the organization's mandate and main concerns. Importantly, it should be noted that the conference is a subsidiary organ of the UNGA and that it serves an important political function: it allows intergovernmental consensus building regarding the state of the world economy and development policies, and ideally plays a key role in identifying the function and responsibilities of the UN and UNCTAD in addressing economic development problems.[15]

UNCTAD's aim—particularly during and immediately after the organization's energetic first head, Raúl Prebisch's tenure (1964–69)—was to address the various issues surrounding the ongoing trade and investment regimes that were felt to hinder development. Indeed, during the height of the South's activism against global inequality (the mid-1970s), UNCTAD led the way as one of the key actors voicing the concerns of the developing world. Promoting an ideological mix of global Keynesianism and dependency theory, the organization urged market intervention to promote development while calling attention to the external and structural constraints on development.[16] For its part, the West was highly ambivalent towards UNCTAD's establishment, preferring to rely upon the GATT to regulate global trading relations.[17] Such a preference suited their own interests, and the developed world's reluctance to discuss substantial issues vis-à-vis development (which threatened to open up all manner of questions regarding the global trading architecture, unequal terms of trade, etc.) manifested itself in the demand to allow decisions made by UNCTAD to be reached by consensus. Such a procedure meant that the terms of the debate and the maneuverability of UNCTAD were constrained from the beginning, with the developed world granted effective influence in line with their material power (thus perpetuating their global dominance over the South), but out of all proportion to their numerical strength. Such structural power enabled the North to "generally confine their role [in UNCTAD] to opposing any proposals for change" while ostensible "positive proposals" of their own were invariably "of a cosmetic nature designed to conceal their underlying resistance to change."[18]

This is not to say that UNCTAD was a doomed body from the start.[19] Indeed, during the epoch surrounding the demand for a NIEO (see below), UNCTAD had some limited success, notably the formulation of the Generalized System of Preferences and the Integrated Program for Commodities. Yet much of the success of such formulations was compromised by the North's unwillingness to fully implement the agreements and "it had become obvious by the late 1970s that the high expectations held in some quarters for progress towards a new order were being frustrated."[20] However, the "structuralism" of Prebisch's theory of "bloodless but inexorable exploitation" inspired a host of impulses from the developing world that emerged in the 1960s and 1970s.[21] These included the Group of 77, the NAM, the OPEC, and the NIEO. All were inspired by first, Bandung, and second, the institutionalization of the post-colonial world's concerns by the establishment of UNCTAD, which during the 1970s and the height of the NIEO moment was the principal vehicle utilized by developing world countries in an attempt to reorganize the global economy.

## The NIEO and UNCTAD

Both UNCTAD and other organizations linked to the developing world reflected not only the growth in membership in the UN of states of the South, but also a steady disillusionment with an ever-apparent unequal world order.[22] This was particularly so as this was an order in which the new states had had no hand in crafting—as Prebisch had made quite explicit. Indeed, UNCTAD was

> . . . the first real confrontation of North and South, symbolic of the new, fundamental structure of international politics, in which the problems of relations of industrialized rich and agricultural poor had replaced the problem of relations between western capitalist and eastern Communist. It was an occasion to redress the injustices perpetrated under colonial regimes.[23]

Thus as the 1970s progressed, the developing world began to push for an agenda that sought to deal with the problems of development. Because the international trading system and the GATT dealt primarily with the promotion of trade between countries of the North, the UN system increasingly became the site where the South pushed for the codification of alternative norms of international trade and promoted agreements that sought to stabilize the prices of primary commodities. As a result of UNCTAD discussions, agreements on a Generalized System of Preferences, providing for lower tariff rates for some exports from the South and on the creation of a Common Fund to help finance buffer stocks for commodity agreements were decided. This concession on the part of the North however was not nearly enough to satisfy the developing world, which pressed for a wide-ranging project that sought to redistribute wealth and begin to unravel the dependent relationships that they saw held them in a subordinate position vis-à-vis the developed world.[24]

UNCTAD thus became an important site of contestation in efforts to put forward the NIEO, sharing a broad *dependencia* worldview.[25] This call for a NIEO symbolically culminated at the Sixth Special Session of the United Nations in 1974 where, under the NAM's then leader (Algeria's Honari Boumedienne), the NAM and G-77 (see p. 38) were successful in pushing for a comprehensive normative declaration detailing the aspirations of the developing world's elites:

> [F]or the first time the General Assembly approved a massive resolution covering all of the economic issues the Third World had raised since the Second World War. The resolution touched on sovereignty over natural resources, improving terms of trade through international regulation of trade based on equitable treatment, reforming the global monetary system to include an aid component, expanding concessionary multilateral aid, providing debt relief, controlling TNCs, promoting international support for industrialization, and reforming the United Nations system to give Third World governments greater control over international economic decisions.[26]

This in essence reflected responses to real problems experienced by states in the post-colonial world, particularly as a result of the Bretton Woods system's creation and operation.[27] It was at the time deemed to be the South "standing up to the world," reflecting "the new mood in the less developed countries."[28]

Emboldened by the demonstration of economic power by the OPEC during the crisis of 1973–74, key elites in the developing world clamored for greater development finance, an increase in the percentage of GNP allocated by the North as aid, and greater representation from the developing world in the specialized multilateral agencies dealing with monetary and development issues, such as the IMF and the International Bank for Reconstruction and Development (IBRD). Overall, these were the heydays of the developing world's role in world affairs as active agents and the NIEO moment put on the international public's agenda development issues as a topic of high concern. It can be said that these were indeed the heydays of UNCTAD too. Thus on the eve of the election to government of conservative neoliberals in the capitalist heartland (i.e. the late 1970s), UNCTAD posited a vision at variance with the gathering thrust of global capitalism and the views of the developed world. The demise of this vision played itself out as an integral part of the reassertion of Western-centered hegemony—"America's quest for supremacy [over] the Third World" and the steady demise (though not outright extinction) of a protesting voice in North-South relations.[29]

At the same time, the failure of Dependency Theory as a grand response to Modernization Theory became evident, with important implications for Prebisch's ideas, as well as UNCTAD's philosophical groundings. A number of factors undermined satisfaction with the *dependencia* account of the global economy. First, and most obviously, the rise of the "Asian Tigers" demonstrated that there was no such thing as a typical underdeveloped country; there were no identical economic and social formations that marked out the developing world—a conundrum that continues today. Indeed, a number of the Tigers actively went against Prebisch's assumptions. After all, according to structuralism, the entry of East Asia into the capitalist global economy should have led to a deepening of underdevelopment, not the opposite.

### *The demise of the NIEO and the rise of another new international economic order: implications for UNCTAD*

The reassertion of dominance by the developed world over the developing world came at a historical juncture when financial indebtedness was acting to drastically undermine—if not emasculate—sovereignty and maneuverability in the developing world. Since formal independence, the developing world had continually borrowed from the North to nurture their economies. With the recycling of petro-dollars making borrowing an easy option with low interest rate repayments, most of the developing world indulged in massive borrowing. Consequently their external debt expanded at a very rapid—and unsustainable—rate. The reckless adventurist lending practices of bankers contributed to this process. However, the massive debts lead to immense problems with such debts creating a vicious Catch-22 situation whereby funds to finance development were diverted to pay off debt. In addition, the necessity to secure foreign currencies to service the debt led to a quick depreciation of many currencies and hyperinflation. Paradoxically, oil prices, which had initially stimulated the lending/borrowing spree exacerbated the problem.

Indeed, as oil prices rose rapidly in the 1970s, most of the developing world felt they were unable to lessen their use of oil for productive purposes and, in order to compensate for the increasing outlay on importing oil, many went deeply into debt. Even countries that produced oil contracted large external debts as the euphoria around the newfound economic power of the oil-producing nations led state elites in countries such as Nigeria and Mexico to believe that the price of oil would continue ever upwards. The decline in oil prices however, produced a huge shortfall between receipts earned by oil exports and the servicing of contracted debt. The OPEC members' usage of Northern banking institutions also resulted in a fatal weakening of the developing world's bargaining position vis-à-vis the North, radically undermining the solidarity that had underpinned both Bandung and the very foundations of UNCTAD.

At the same time, leadership fractions within the developing world were increasingly drawn into an ongoing restructuring process. Indeed, the call for liberalization—dressed up as it was in the rhetoric of economic "realities"—gave space for conservative elements within the ruling elites, many of whom had always been reluctant to concretely commit themselves to the NIEO. Their seizure upon the growing right-wing discourse to help explain away unpopular policies to cope with the debt crises reflected a long-standing minimal commitment to any major restructuring of the global economy. This, combined with an ever-increasing consensus among elites over the liberalization of economic policies, meant that "alternative" visions regarding the international political economy were conceived as largely redundant among elite circles. Confrontationist expressions, which had been omnipresent in much of UNCTAD's rhetoric in the 1960s and 1970s, were now deemed incongruous in a world where there was "no alternative" to neoliberalism. Impulses generated by Prebisch's insights gave way to what was essentially a return to Modernization Theory with the imposition of Structural Adjustment Programs (SAPs).[30]

The era of SAPs advanced a dual strategy for development in the South: privatization and liberalization. Reform packages that were rolled out in the 1980s by all the main creditors as well as donors contained these two basic elements as essential conditionalities for disbursements. A structural adjustment package, granted in 1981 to Côte d'Ivoire and soon to become the first of what would eventually become 26 SAPs to that country, captures the basic ingredients:

> The reforms envisaged by the program are designed to improve the level of public savings and the efficiency in the use of public resources; restructure the agricultural planning system and associated development institutions so that an expanded, well-designed investment program yielding high returns can be mounted in the sector; reflect the costs of providing public services to the sector; assure that rational prices and world market conditions would guide decisions to invest and produce; restructure public enterprise, management, financing and accountability to ensure efficient market oriented operations; restructure incentives, to promote efficient export-oriented industrial investments.[31]

These elements staked out both an economic and political project and came at a historical juncture when financial indebtedness and economic mismanagement were acting to drastically undermine the South's development trajectory. Equally, the NIEO was actively attacked by the North, with American economists such as Martin Bronfenbrenner dismissing the NIEO as "a conspiracy or lunacy" being advanced Mafia-style by the South and akin to fascism.[32] Such hysterical and unbalanced outbursts did however bolster the position of the ascending neoliberal elements within the Northern elites who believed that the NIEO was an "unreasonable" demand on their power and interests—something which had to be crushed.

Furthermore, as the debt crisis worsened, growth stagnated, employment declined, monetary arrangements collapsed and financial agreements between creditors and debtors were increasingly undermined by mass bankruptcies. In short, the room for maneuver by Southern elites became more and more constricted.[33] The means to overcome the crisis was by borrowing from two old theoretical approaches: neoclassical economics, and Modernization Theory.[34] This combination was part and parcel of the SAPs that reconfigured whole swathes of the developing world in the 1980s. Within SAPs was an implicit echoing of the modernizers' argument that the "fundamentals" had to be in place to assure economic development. Failure to do this, particularly by African states, was blamed for the failure of SAPs in many countries.[35]

It was in this context that the elites within bodies such as UNCTAD sought to restructure the organization. Certainly, while the logic of neoliberalism was broadly accepted by most, its negative effects were equally felt. An acceptance of the normative principles of neoliberalism, while advocating ameliorating policies to cope with this "actuality" emerged as defining principles upon which the organization now operated. This will be discussed in greater detail below as the book progresses. At this point, however, it is necessary to take a step back and discuss and analyze the organizational structure of UNCTAD. In doing so, the way in which the organization operates and produces output is explained, as is the role of the Secretariat and the secretary-general. Given that the Secretariat is central to UNCTAD's existence, coverage of this body is essential in order to place the structure of the organization within its historical setting.

# 2 UNCTAD's Secretariat structure

As the previous chapter has demonstrated, UNCTAD's Secretariat is central to the organization's management and operations. Permanently based in Geneva it is where the day-to-day running of the body is carried out, as well as from where the research—arguably UNCTAD's key comparative advantage over other bodies—is conducted and marshaled. Consequently, this chapter will discuss in depth the structure of the Secretariat, what it does and how, and how the overall organization fits together. The chapter also discusses the evolution of the Secretariat over time. The following chapter (Chapter 3) will then discuss the research activities of UNCTAD and the importance of its publications and reports.

## Overview of the Secretariat

The day-to-day work of the organization is undertaken by the UNCTAD Secretariat. Located in Geneva and with a staff of about 400, it forms part of the United Nations (UN) Secretariat. Taking a brief look at the structure and division of work within the Secretariat will provide us with an overview of the activities that UNCTAD is involved in. This will lay the foundation for a more detailed discussion of the evolution of the organization's mandate, and the challenges it has faced. The Secretariat's main functions can be divided into the following sub-headings:

- research, analysis and dissemination of information;
- practical policy advice;
- technical assistance and capacity building;
- consensus building through intergovernmental meetings.

Since the founding of the organization in 1964, the organizational structure of the Secretariat has kept pace with the changing nature and focus of UNCTAD's work, within the broader context of a changing global environment. The most far-reaching reforms were undertaken in 1995, when the entire Secretariat was restructured under the leadership of the new secretary-general, Rubens Ricupero. The previously existing nine divisions were regrouped into four, according to subject matter, and a special co-coordinator was appointed to ensure that special attention is given to the needs of the least developed countries (LDCs). This restructuring eventually resulted in the current Secretariat structure, consisting of five functional divisions, of which four are engaged in research and technical assistance, and the fifth is tasked with general management and intergovernmental affairs. In addition, there is a Special Program dealing specifically with the unique challenges faced by the least developed, landlocked and small island developing states.

In executing their mandates, the divisions work in close cooperation with member states, and liaise with other UN bodies, intergovernmental and nongovernmental organizations, private sector associations and a variety of research institutes. This chapter provides a brief outline of the main functions of each of the Secretariat's divisions.

## Globalization and development strategies (GDS)

This division is charged with conducting research into and analyzing global economic trends, especially as they affect developing states. UNCTAD's work on development strategies since the mid-1980s can be understood within the context of the search for a new development paradigm in line with emerging issues in the global environment.[1] An important part of this is examining the impact of globalization, and how it can be managed to promote rather than impede development.

Another major part of its work involves providing countries with assistance in the areas of external debt management and (re-)integration into the international financial system. Beyond these short-term measures to individual countries, the division also examines the broader issue of developing world debt, and how this might be solved. The causes and impacts of financial crises form another research focus, with the division proposing strategies for the prevention and management of these crises. In doing so, it relies greatly on identifying successful development strategies in developing states and economies in transition that can be replicated elsewhere.

There is also a special focus on the development challenges facing Africa, with the division participating in implementing the United Nations New Agenda for the Development of Africa (UN-NADAF).

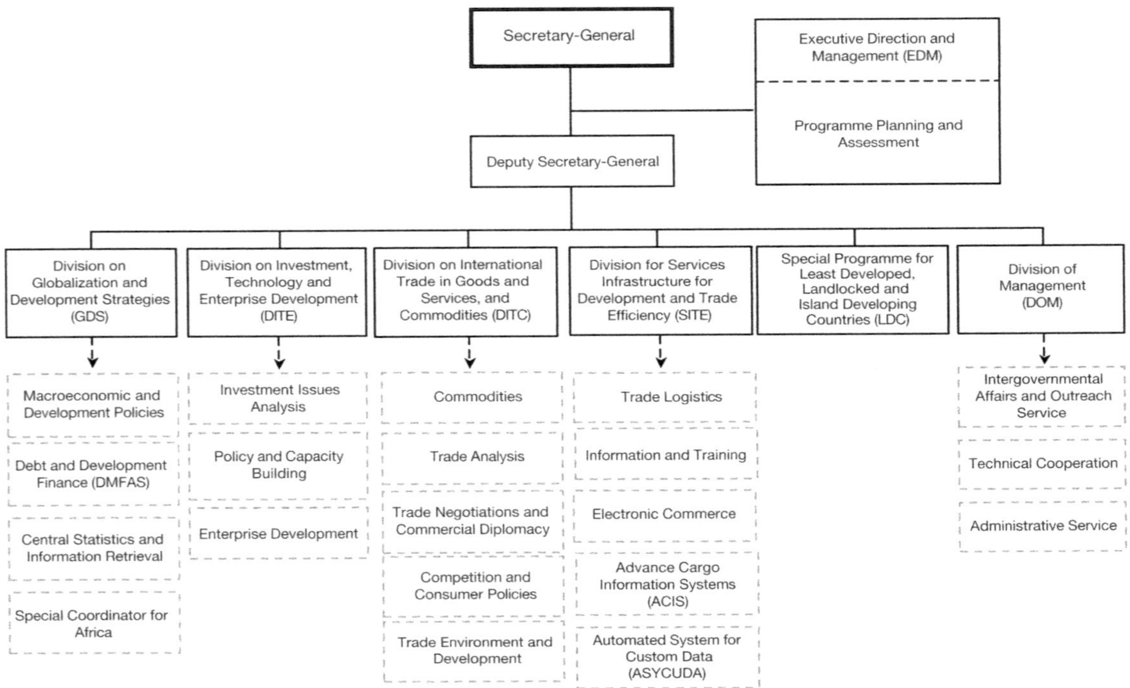


*Figure 1* The UNCTAD Secretariat.

In 2005, it published a new *Report on Economic Development in Africa*, focusing on the issue of foreign direct investment (FDI), and the prominent role it has assumed in the continent's economic development strategies. The report warns that the focus by African states on implementing reforms aimed at improving their investment climate and attracting FDI has been at the expense of due consideration of the costs and benefits that FDI brings with it. It proposes a more critical approach to FDI that takes into account Africa's unique development challenges.

Finally, the division is responsible for publishing UNCTAD's annual *Trade and Development Report*, and is also the seat of the organization's statistical office. The Secretariat's research, analysis and publications will be discussed in more detail in the following chapter.

## Division on International Trade in Goods and Services, and Commodities (DITC)

The DITC's work is premised on the idea that international trade should be the main mechanism through which developing countries can develop. With this aim in mind, the division aims to manage and find solutions to the challenges faced by developing states in integrating into and benefiting from the global trade system. It does so by focusing on areas including trade in goods and services, commodities, competition policies and the relationship between trade and the environment.

Although the Secretariat has always been active in analyzing developments in the international trading system, its work on trade and development took on an increasing importance at the beginning of the 1990s when it became clear that one of the results of the Uruguay Round would most likely be the establishment of a new institution to replace the GATT. Since the birth of the World Trade Organization (WTO), the DITC has played an important role in examining how its activities impact on developing countries.

An important part of the Secretariat's work has been providing technical support to and assisting developing countries in enhancing their bargaining position in multilateral trade negotiations. This has included offering analysis of competition law and policy to assist developing states in dealing with the challenges of market access and competitiveness. Part of this effort was the Secretariat's implementation of the Positive Agenda for Trade Negotiations in 1997, a program aimed at turning around the defensive and reactive position most developing countries took in trade negotiations to a more proactive one. In light of UNCTAD's focus on capacity building, the program did more than simply provide expert advice to these countries. Instead, through the provision of training and analytical tools, it encouraged developing countries to develop technically and legally strong, independent negotiating positions, based on their particular needs and conditions.[2]

The DITC places special emphasis on the role that trade in commodities can play in development. Commodities have been at the heart of UNCTAD's trade and development agenda since its inception.[3] This is largely due to the central role that commodities have played, and continue to play, in the national economies of many developing, and especially least developing, countries. Concern about this dependence on commodities was one of the main driving forces leading to the UN General Assembly's decision to create UNCTAD in 1964.

Over the years, the Secretariat has, most recently through the DITC, conducted research and analysis into the commodities sector, and proposed solutions to developing countries having to deal with problems like commodity price fluctuations. In addition, the Secretariat has also assisted countries in multilateral trade negotiations on commodities, with the overall aim of achieving economic growth and development goals through the commodity sector.

Another part of the capacity-building activities on trade-related matters for developing countries provided by the division includes assisting states in improving their export capabilities, and strengthening their service sector capabilities. Services were not always regarded as having an important role to play in the development process. As Kasahara points out, "The conventional theory of the role of services in the national economy tended to suggest that growth in the services sector was a result of the development process."[4] This changed in the early 1980s, when debates on the service sector were conducted in a broader developmental context, and trade in services was added as a new issue in the 1982 GATT Ministerial meeting. UNCTAD was mandated to conduct a study on the role of service in the development process. The outcome was a major study, entitled *Services and the Development Process*,[5] which challenged the view that service sector growth is a result of the development process; instead arguing that "the former could be one of the preconditions for the latter."[6] This led to services being regarded as key economic activities in their own right, and the importance of public investment in services became an increasingly important subject for research and analysis. This opened up "a whole new area of intellectual activities in the UNCTAD Secretariat."[7]

Prior to and during the Uruguay Round, a number of studies on trade in services were produced by the Secretariat. One of the outputs was a book entitled *Trade in Services: Sectoral Issues*,[8] which found that developing countries could benefit from the liberalization of trade in services, from improved access to producer services, improved service infrastructure and from more open markets for their service exports. At the same time, given the tremendous employment opportunities of the service industry, countries were cautioned to carefully consider the wider impacts of liberalization.[9]

Initially, the Secretariat adopted a holistic approach to researching and analyzing the service sector, instead of concentrating on specific sub-sectors. At the same time, the framework of analysis used focused on the relationship between services and development rather than services and trade. Following UNCTAD VIII (1992), however, the holistic approach was replaced by a specialized functional approach, with studies done on specific sectors like tourism.[10]

Finally, besides its focus on the link between trade and development, the division also promotes an integrated approach to trade, development and the environment. Relatedly, it does work on the particular environmental challenges faced by developing states. In fact, UNCTAD was the first organization to initiate empirical work on trade and environment linkages, and UNCTAD submitted a report on "Environment and International Trade" to the United Nations Conference on Environment and Development (UNCED) in 1991. In addition, the Secretariat's work has also provided a basis for Agenda 21, which was adopted at the Earth Summit in 1992.

## Division on Investment, Technology, and Enterprise Development (DITE)

The division's work has three overarching objectives, which it aims to achieve through an integrated approach.[11] The first relates to enhancing the understanding of the role that foreign direct investment, technology and enterprise-related activities can play, particularly in developing countries, in the development process. The second involves assisting developing countries in improving their investment climate and implementing policies ensuring developmental benefits from investment, as well as facilitating technology transfer and diffusion. The final objective forms part of the Secretariat's broader aim of building consensus, especially through its intergovernmental machinery, on the issues mentioned above. Each of the issue areas that the division focuses on will briefly be discussed in turn.

### *Investment*

Although the organization was initially established with a focus on trade, since the early 1990s UNCTAD has become the central organization in the UN system dealing with issues relating to FDI and transnational corporations (TNCs). After UNCTAD VIII (1992), the Secretariat was mandated with facilitating the understanding of the nature of TNCs and their contribution to development, and "for creating an enabling environment for international investment and enterprise development through research, policy analysis, technical assistance and consensus building."[12] Prior to this, work on TNCs was conducted at the United Nations Center on Transnational Corporations (UNCTC), which was established in 1974 when the importance of these powerful corporations in the global economy became increasingly obvious.[13] In 1993, the responsibilities of the Commission on Transnational Corporations, to which the UNCTC reported, were transferred from New York to UNCTAD's offices in Geneva.

With its focus on one of the cornerstones of UNCTAD's overall objectives, the DITE helps developing countries—in particular the LDCs—devise investment strategies that will make an impact on development. Part of the division's work in this regard is of an academic nature: researching and analyzing global FDI trends, and compiling data on FDI. All the information collected and generated by the DITE is disseminated through e-discussion forums, e-research notes and online databases and tools. UNCTAD's Global Investment Prospects Assessment (GIPA), which is designed to assess future patterns of FDI flows, is one such statistical tool.[14]

Through this work, the division has been instrumental in promoting the development of new concepts and approaches to analyzing data in order to promote a better understanding of FDI and TNC activities. As Fredriksson and Zimny[15] contend, "The thinking and development-oriented work of UNCTAD on foreign direct investment (FDI) and transnational corporations (TNCs) has moved from a marginal position on UNCTAD's agenda to a key area of work in which the organization has earned a strong reputation for contributing to mainstream thinking on the subject." In this way, UNCTAD has been an important role player in the debate around the benefits versus the drawbacks of FDI.

UNCTAD's perspective on the role of FDI in development has also kept pace with changing perceptions in the developing world. When the topic first appeared on the UNCTAD agenda in the 1970s, the attitude of the organization and the developing world was very critical. Initially, the work of the UNCTC focused on studying TNCs from a critical perspective, and on helping developing countries in dealing with the negative impacts of TNCs. This changed in the late 1980s, when interest turned to the positive impact of FDI and TNCs—with TNCs now being seen as part of the solution instead of part of the problem. The first few issues of the *World Investment Report* (*WIR*), which UNCTAD started publishing in 1991,[16] reflect this new conviction that investment by TNCs is imperative to the economic growth and development of the poorest countries.

Based on its research work, the DITE has provided policy advice to developing countries and intergovernmental organizations regarding optimal policies to pursue in order to reap the most developmental benefits from FDI and TNCs. It also plays an advisory role in providing practical policy advice to countries wanting to enhance their ability to attract foreign direct investment and improve their national and international investment policymaking and negotiation capacity. This includes the development of tools for analyzing economic and policy factors that impact on the investment environment. In 2005, the division was involved in about 120 advisory missions, which included training services and assisting in strengthening the role of individual countries' investment promotion agencies (IPAs).[17]

In response to the proliferation of international investment agreements (IIAs) during the 1990s, the Secretariat stepped in to provide advice and assistance to governments lacking expertise in this field. As Fredriksson and Zimny (2004: 132) point out, while negotiators from developing countries were becoming increasingly adept at trade negotiations, the complex investment policy concepts and their development implications were unfamiliar territory.

The 1990s also saw the Secretariat expanding its technical assistance program in the area of investment to include a series of *Investment Policy Reviews (IPRs)* and *Investment Guides for LDCs*. The *Reviews* are aimed at helping developing countries to assess and improve their investment climate, while the *Guides* which provide reports on the progress made by LDCs in improving their investment environment, are a valuable resource for potential investors. In addition, the first series of *International Investment Agreements* (IIA), the aim of which is to assist developing countries in participating effectively in international rule setting for investment, was completed during 2005. Besides these publications, the DITE's flagship publication is the *World Investment Report*, which has become an authoritative source on FDI and development, and which will be discussed in greater detail in the following chapter. The division is also responsible for publishing the journal *Transnational Corporations*, which contains policy-oriented articles examining the impacts of TNCs and FDI.

### *Science and technology*

While issues relating to technology were identified as being a core part of UNCTAD's work at its inception in 1964, it was only at UNCTAD II (1968) that the transfer and diffusion of technology, and its relationship to trade and development, was afforded serious attention.

It is possible to identify three main reasons why technology, which until the late 1960s was seen as an issue of national policy, was increasingly regarded as an issue of importance to an intergovernmental organization like UNCTAD.[18] The first was a realization of how crucial technology is to advancing economic growth, and ultimately, development. The second and third reasons concerned the impact of the technological gap and the cost of technology transfer between the developed and developing world. UNCTAD's initial focus was thus on facilitating technology transfer to developing countries. Here the Secretariat's research and analysis work was instrumental in conceptualizing the technology transfer issue, and identifying constraints to improving access to technology.

Over the past two decades, however, there has been a shift from a focus on technology transfer to a concern about the significance of technology diffusion and capacity building. According to Omer, Soubra and Konde[19] the shift in approach was due to the "recognition that technology transfer is a more complex process than previously assumed, where the transfer occurs not only in a one-way direction from developed to developing countries but in a multi-directional and multi-dimensional fashion involving enterprises of all sizes." In addition, technology transfer increasingly became seen not as an end in itself, but as a way to expand national technological capacity and competitiveness. To this end, the Secretariat conducted a range of analytical and policy-related work, including case studies on technological problems in specific industries, with the aim of assisting developing countries to improve their technology environment.

Since the 1990s, the Secretariat's work on technology became increasingly prominent, largely due to the fact that a number of international agreements on technology transfer to developing countries were completed, and the Secretariat carried out studies to assess the implications of these agreements. In addition, the UN Center for Science and Technology was moved from New York to Geneva, and the responsibility for servicing the United Nations Commission on Science and Technology for Development (CSTD) fell to the UNCTAD Secretariat. It was also charged with assessing the policy implications of the WTO's Agreement on Trade Related Aspects of Intellectual Property Rights (TRIPS) on developing countries.[20]

One of the division's main outputs in the area of science and technology are its Science, Technology and Innovation Policy (STIP) reviews for developing countries in order to evaluate their national policies in these fields, and to help governments formulate new policies that will address their development goals.

The DITE is also directly involved in promoting technology transfer through FDI and implementing capacity-building programs in developing countries to encourage the use of new technologies. An example of its work in this field is the recently launched Network of Centers of Excellence in Science and Technology, which are aimed at "helping to bridge the North-South technology gap by creating regional learning hubs, encouraging the exchange of knowledge and reversing the current 'brain-drain' affecting developing countries."[21]

In cooperation with the International Center on Trade and Sustainable Development (ICTSD), the WTO and the World Intellectual Property Organization (WIPO), the DITE has also examined the relationship between technology transfer and intellectual property. It has played an important role in advising developing countries on the legal framework of technology transfer, and ensuring the fairness of international technology transactions.

### *Enterprise competitiveness*

The third and final focus area of the DITE is the promotion of enterprise competitiveness, particularly aimed at the development of micro, small and medium-sized enterprises (SMEs). The rationale for this focus is the belief that through engaging in international trade and investment alone, countries may not be able to achieve their development goals. An important component of development is nurturing a robust enterprise sector, which enables a country to take advantage of trade and investment opportunities. To this effect, the division provides advisory services to countries to build their institutional capacity in order to assist their enterprises to survive and compete in the global economy and to participate in mutually beneficial business linkages with TNCs.

## Division of Services Infrastructure for Development and Trade Efficiency (SITE)

The objective of this division is to facilitate international trade by improving the operation of trade-supporting services, particularly in developing countries. There is also a special emphasis on addressing the challenges faced by landlocked and transit developing countries. SITE's aims are achieved largely though the division's strong technical assistance component, which provides support, capacity building and training to developing countries and economies in transition in a number of trade facilitation issues, including transport, customs procedures, the improved use of information technologies and management systems, and e-commerce.

Given that shipping is the major form of transport used in world trade, this division has been concerned with ensuring access to affordable maritime transport for developing countries. This has been compounded by a number of decisions taken by major maritime countries, which have hampered the development of developing country fleets. Despite these constraints, SITE has, through its research and support to developing countries, been able to exert considerable influence over the negotiations and decisions taken by governments on this issue. In terms of its general policy angle, the division has pushed for developing country governments to adopt a more interventionist policy in developing their national fleets.[22]

Specific programs recently implemented by the division include UNCTAD's E-Tourism Initiative, which is concerned with the use of information and communication technologies in promoting tourism. In particular, it focuses on the role the Internet can play in shifting profits from tourism from multinational tour operators to providers based in developing countries.

The division is also responsible for the publication of the annual *E-Commerce and Development Report,* which analyses trends in information and communications technologies (ICTs) and their potential development impact on developing countries, and the *Review of Maritime Transport*.

## Special Program for Least Developed, Landlocked and Small Island Developing Countries (LDCs, LLDCs, and SIDS)

It was Raúl Prebisch, the first secretary-general of UNCTAD, who first called on the international community to recognize the differences between developing countries in considering international support measures to these countries. Ever since, the UNCTAD Secretariat has advocated for special and differential treatment of different developing countries, depending on their level of development and other relevant criteria. A large part of its work has also involved developing and finding ways to measure these criteria.[23]

There has always been a special unit in the Secretariat dealing with the least developed, landlocked and island developing countries. Initially, during the late 1960s, a section of the former Research Division was charged with this task. Between 1977 and 1992 its work was taken over by the Special Program for Least Developed, Landlocked and Island Developing Countries (LDCs, LLDCs, and SIDS), which underwent a number of transformations—becoming the Division for Least Developed, Landlocked and Island Developing Countries between 1992 and 1996, then the Office of the Special Coordinator for Least Developed, Landlocked and Island Developing Countries between 1996 and 2001, and eventually the Special Program on the Least Developed Countries, Landlocked and Island Developing Countries.[24]

An important aspect of the Special Program's work is to help these countries to capitalize on this recognition, and the accompanying special international support measures that they have been accorded. These include measures aimed at reducing their marginalization in the global economy, improving their infrastructure, developing human resources and institutional capacities, and providing support to LDCs, LLDCs and SIDS in developing common positions towards international issues which affect them all. UNCTAD's work in this regard has culminated in three UN Conferences on the Least Developed Countries (Paris, 1981;[25] Paris, 1990 and Brussels, 2001), aiming to focus the attention of the international community on the problems of LDCs. The outcome of each of the conferences has been the adoption of a decennial program of action for LDCs. The most recent Program of Action for LDCs for 2001–10 serves to coordinate UNCTAD's work on the LDCs, the LLDCs and the small island developing states (SIDS). Its overarching goal is "to make substantial progress towards halving the proportion of people living in extreme poverty."[26]

Over the past decades, the Secretariat has played an important role in assisting these countries to develop national policies aimed at transforming their economies within the context of different international policy frameworks. Initially, the focus was on national planning as the key instrument in economic management. This was followed by the era of stabilization and structural adjustment programs (SAPs), which called for a different approach. Recently, UNCTAD has been assisting LDCs in making policy changes within the context of the Poverty Reduction Strategy Paper (PRSP) process.[27]

The UNCTAD Secretariat's analytical work on trade policy issues relevant to LDCs has mainly focused on market access, international commodity policies and supply capacities. In terms of market access, the Secretariat recommended that particular measures which would benefit LDCs be added to existing preferential schemes granted to developing countries. With regard to commodities, the Secretariat's work has focused on extending the special conditions for LDCs' participation in international commodity agreements. The Secretariat has also been very involved in supporting LDCs in capacity building, including expanding infrastructure, implementing diversification programs, improving competitiveness, and identifying development objectives.[28] In addition, in light of the importance the UNCTAD Secretariat places on the role that people skills can play in economic growth and development, much work has gone into advising LDCs on how to invest in human resource development by strengthening educational and vocational training policies.

While considerable effort has been put into maximizing the capacities of LDCs to address their problems, the Secretariat has always emphasized the fact that these countries would not be able to pull themselves out of their positions of marginalization, underdevelopment and poverty without international support measures. Related to this has been the compounding problem of debt service payments, which has resulted in the Secretariat calling for a more effective international debt relief strategy.[29]Although the three categories of countries falling under this Special Program—the LDCs, the LLDCs and the SIDS—have many similarities with regard to their marginalization in the global economy, there are also important differences between them which the Special Program has taken in consideration in developing strategies to assist these countries.

UNCTAD has played a leading role in mobilizing international support for the LDCs, which face great challenges in addressing poverty and underdevelopment. The Special Program is engaged in a number of activities aimed at assisting the LDCs in their efforts to better integrate their economies in the multilateral trading system. These include the provision of technical assistance, particularly through the Integrated Framework (IF) for Trade-related Technical Assistance to LDCs.

LLDCs face severe challenges to growth and development due to a wide range of factors. In addition to poor physical infrastructure, weak institutional and productive capacities, small domestic markets, and a high vulnerability to external shocks, they have added transit problems that come with being landlocked. The Special Program is involved in developing strategies for improving national transport networks, promoting regional or sub-regional economic integration, and encouraging foreign direct investment in economic activities that are not distance-sensitive.

SIDS are believed to be at a greater risk of marginalization from the global economy than many other developing countries due to their small size, remoteness from large markets, and high economic vulnerability to economic and natural disasters beyond domestic control. In addition, their fragile ecosystems make them more vulnerable to pollution and climatic changes such as rising sea levels. Working within the framework of the Program of Action, the UNCTAD Secretariat has provided technical assistance targeted at addressing the unique challenges faced by these different categories of poor countries.

In conclusion, UNCTAD's work on LDCs has become increasingly important in the context of the UN's Millennium Development Goals, and the realization that the eradication of extreme poverty remains one of the greatest challenges of our age.

## Division of Management (DOM)

One of the Secretariat's main functions remains the provision of administrative and technical support to the intergovernmental meetings that take place under the auspices of UNCTAD. Since its founding in 1964, the Secretariat has provided support to 11 UNCTAD sessions and three United Nations Conferences on the Least Developed Countries. The division tasked with the overall coordination of the Secretariat's support functions is the DOM, which consists of the Administrative Service, the Technical Cooperation Services and the Intergovernmental Affairs and Outreach Service.

As has been noted, one of the UNCTAD Secretariat's main functions is its research and analysis work. Annually, the various divisions of the Secretariat publish a number of reports, reviews, and statistics which developing countries, academics, research institutions and the international community at large have come to rely on heavily. The Secretariat's efforts in this area will be explored in the following chapter.

## The role of the secretary-general

The secretary-general of UNCTAD is appointed by the secretary-general of the UN, and this appointment is authorized by the General Assembly. There is a defined manner by which a new secretary-general is chosen. The retiring secretary-general is asked to draw up a list of three possible candidates, one from each continent that is composed of primarily developing countries. The secretary-general of the UN then selects a candidate. This person will be, as a rule, from a continent different from where the retiring secretary-general hails from, unless a candidate emerges from the same continent who may be a particularly strong and compelling choice. Thus far, there have been six secretaries-general, three of whom have come from Latin America: Raúl Prebisch (Argentina), 1963–9; Manuel Pérez-Guerrero (Venezuela), 1969–74; Gamani Corea (Sri Lanka), 1974–84; Kenneth Dadzie (Ghana), 1986–94; Rubens Ricupero (Brazil), 1995–2004; Supachai Panitchpakdi (Thailand), 2005–present.

The secretary-general heads the UNCTAD Secretariat, which executes the work required to organize the various conferences that the organization undertakes, as well as the numerous analyses and reports that make up UNCTAD's bread and butter. The structure of UNCTAD means that the secretary-general is highly influential in shaping the dynamics and overall posture of the organization. A brief biographical sketch of each secretary-general thus far follows.

### *Box 2.1* UNCTAD secretaries-general, 1964–2006

#### *Dr Raúl Prebisch (1964–1969)*

Raúl Prebisch was born in 1901 in Argentina. He studied Economics at the University of Buenos Aires from 1918 to 1922 and worked as Professor of Economic Policy at the Faculty of Economic Sciences, National University of Buenos Aires, 1923–48. Whilst a professor he also held various positions in the public sector, as Deputy Director of the Argentine Department of Statistics (1925–7), Director of Economic Research for the National Bank of Argentina (1927–30), Under-Secretary of Finance (1930–2) and first Director-General of the Argentine Central Bank (1935–48). Prebisch entered service with the Economic Commission for Latin America (ECLA), acting as the Executive Secretary from 1950 to 1963.[30] He then served as secretary-general of UNCTAD from 1964 to 1969. Prebisch's tenure as secretary-general was marked with high enthusiasm and energy for a fairer international economic order and Prebisch's writings on development economics helped form the Dependency School of economic theory. Prebisch died in Chile in April 1986.

### *Manuel Pérez-Guerrero (1969–1974)*

Manuel Pérez-Guerrero was born in 1911 in Venezuela and started his international diplomatic career with the League of Nations in the 1930s, later holding various senior positions within the United Nations (UN) system. He was appointed secretary-general of UNCTAD from 1969 to 1974. Pérez-Guerrero was also a senior government official in his home country of Venezuela and held ministerial positions in Finance, Planning, Mines and Hydrocarbons and International Economic Affairs. He was instrumental in the formation of OPEC and hosted a variety of important North-South and South-South conferences as well as the Group of 77. Pérez-Guerrero died in 1985.

### *Gamani Corea (1974–1984)*

Gamani Corea is a graduate of the University of Ceylon and Cambridge University and holds a DPhil in Economics from Oxford University. Whilst in his native Sri Lanka he was employed at the Planning Secretariat, the Ministry of Planning and Economic Affairs, the Bank of Ceylon and was Sri Lanka's Ambassador to the EEC and Benelux countries in 1973. He had been involved in helping to set up UNCTAD I back in 1964 and was the Chairman of UNCTAD's Expert Groups on International Monetary Issues in 1965 and 1969, as well as the Chairman of the UN's Cocoa Conference in 1972. Upon stepping down as UNCTAD's secretary-general, Corea was Chairman of the Board of the South Center in Geneva, Switzerland, 2002–2003 and authored books on development issues.

### *Kenneth Dadzie (1986–1994)*

Dadzie was born in 1930 and worked as a diplomat in Ghana's diplomatic service, 1952–1985. During this time he was placed on secondment to the UN Secretariat in Geneva and New York. He was appointed as Ghana's permanent representative to the United Nations Office in Geneva while also Ambassador to Austria and Switzerland. Dadzie was appointed secretary-general in 1986. He was influential in the adoption of the Final Act of UNCTAD VII and at UNCTAD VIII, the "Spirit of Cartagena." Dadzie died in October 1995 in London.

***Rubens Ricupero (1995–2004)***

Rubens Ricupero was born in Sao Paulo, Brazil in 1937. He was Minister of the Environment and Amazonian Affairs and later Minister of Finance (1994), as well as Ambassador and permanent representative to the UN in Geneva (1987–1991), Ambassador to the United States of America (1991–1993) and Ambassador to Italy (1995). He also chaired various councils and committees at the GATT between 1989 and 1991. He was appointed UNCTAD's fifth secretary-general in 1995 and reappointed for another four-year term in 1999.

***Dr Supachai Panitchpakdi (2005–)***

Born in Bangkok in 1946, Dr Supachai began his career at the Bank of Thailand in 1974, working in the Research Department, the International Finance Division and the Financial Institution's Supervision Department. In 1986, Dr Supachai was elected a member of the Thai Parliament and was appointed Deputy Minister of Finance, being appointed Director and Advisor in 1988, subsequently becoming President of the Thai Military Bank. In 1992, Dr Supachai was appointed Senator, and that same year he became Deputy Prime Minister. In this role he represented Thailand at the signing ceremony in Marrakech of the Uruguay Round Agreement in 1994. He was also active in shaping regional agreements, including Asia Pacific Economic Cooperation (APEC), the Association of Southeast Asian Nations (ASEAN) and the Asia Europe Meeting (ASEM). In September 1999, he was elected Director-General of the World Trade Organization (WTO), taking office on 1 September 2002.

While the Secretary-General provides leadership, member nations within UNCTAD behave as per the group system within the ministerial meetings. This is the basis upon which positions are generally made and an analysis of this follows.

## The UNCTAD group system

Within UNCTAD each state member is allotted one vote and at the ministerial conferences, substantive resolutions need a two-thirds majority of those in attendance (procedural motions need only a simple majority). It should be pointed out that since the late 1980s, UNCTAD's decisions have not been made by votes. Agreements are typically worked out in informal consultations. However, UNCTAD functions on the basis of the group system, and this is the main way decisions are made at UNCTAD's meetings. At UNCTAD I in 1964, 77 developing countries came together as the Group of 77 (see Box 2.2). The G-77 was established by signatories to the "Joint Declaration of the Seventy-Seven Countries" issued at the close of UNCTAD I. The Group's first Ministerial Meeting was in Algiers in 1967. A permanent institutional framework slowly emerged, leading to the formation of Chapters of the G-77, such as the Rome-based Food and Agriculture Organization (FAO), United Nations Environment Programme (UNEP) in Nairobi, United Nations Educational, Scientific and Cultural Organization (UNESCO) in Paris, and the United Nations Industrial Development Organization (UNIDO) in Vienna. As the biggest coalition of developing nations within UN structures, the G-77 brings together a diverse membership. The Ministerial Meeting acts as the top decision-making structure, convened annually at the start of sessions of the UNGA, and regularly before UNCTAD sessions and the General Conferences of both UNESCO and UNIDO.

Initially, UNCTAD members were divided into four groups based on geography and socioeconomic status. This was done to facilitate the election of representatives to the Trade and Development Board (TDB). The groupings were as follows:

1 Group A was made up of the African and Asian state members and Yugoslavia. They were allocated 22 seats on the TDB.
2 Group B was composed of the developed countries with market economies and was also allocated 22 seats.
3 Group C was made up of the Latin American and Caribbean countries and was given nine seats on the TDB.
4 Group D consisted of the socialist countries of Eastern Europe and was allocated six seats.

It was Groups A and C that combined to form the G-77. What this has meant in practice is that historically there have been three active groups, rather than four (although after the collapse of the socialist countries, Group D ceased functioning). Until its demise, Group D generally supported the G-77 within UNCTAD.

It should be pointed out that after China replaced Taiwan in 1971, Beijing adopted a notionally independent position and is not a formal member of the G-77. However, it invariably sides with the Group.

### *Box 2.2* G-77 members

Afghanistan
Algeria
Angola
Antigua and Barbuda
Argentina
Bahamas
Bahrain
Bangladesh
Barbados
Belize
Benin
Bhutan
Bolivia
Bosnia and Herzegovina
Botswana
Brazil
Brunei Darussalam
Burkina Faso
Burundi
Cambodia
Cameroon
Cape Verde
Central African Republic
Chad
Chile
China
Colombia
Comoros
Congo
Costa Rica
Côte d'Ivoire
Cuba
DR Congo
Djibouti
Dominica
Dominican Republic
Ecuador
Egypt
El Salvador
Equatorial Guinea
Eritrea
Ethiopia
Fiji
Gabon
Gambia
Ghana
Grenada
Guatemala
Guinea
Guinea-Bissau
Guyana
Haiti
Honduras
India
Indonesia
Iran
Iraq
Jamaica
Jordan
Kenya
Kuwait
Laos
Lebanon
Lesotho
Liberia
Libya
Madagascar
Malawi
Malaysia
Maldives
Mali
Marshall Islands
Mauritania
Mauritius
Federated States of Micronesia
Mongolia
Morocco
Mozambique
Myanmar
Namibia
Nepal
Nicaragua
Niger
Nigeria
North Korea
Oman
Pakistan
Palau
Palestine
Panama
Papua New Guinea
Paraguay
Peru
Philippines
Qatar
Romania
Rwanda
St. Kitts and Nevis
St. Lucia
St. Vincent and Grenadines
Samoa
São Tomé and Príncipe
Saudi Arabia
Senegal
Seychelles
Sierra Leone
Singapore
Solomon Islands
Somalia

| | | |
|---|---|---|
| South Africa | Togo | Uruguay |
| Sri Lanka | Tonga | Vanuatu |
| Sudan | Trinidad and Tobago | Venezuela |
| Suriname | Tunisia | Viet Nam |
| Swaziland | Turkmenistan | Yemen |
| Syria | Uganda | Zambia |
| Tanzania | United Arab Emirates | Zimbabwe |
| Timor-Leste | | |
| Thailand | | |

In formal meetings of UNCTAD the G-77 spokesperson usually prefaces G-77 statements with the acknowledgment that the statement is on behalf of the member states of the Group of 77 *and* China. Chinese spokespeople take the floor separately from the African, Asian or Latin American delegates. As mentioned, votes are not taken within UNCTAD these days and so the term "resolutions" is rarely used—most decisions are made on a consensus basis. In 1994 a Joint Coordinating Committee (JCC) of the G-77 and NAM was established, based in New York. As mentioned previously, the NAM was officially launched in 1961 at a summit in the Yugoslav capital Belgrade, held at the instigation of Yugoslav President Tito. At Belgrade a declaration containing the common views of delegates on international problems was issued. The NAM committed itself to a project that privileged the role of the UN as the proper forum for interstate activity. NAM also expressed a desire by a large number of states to operate in a world less beholden to the unilateralist activities of the superpowers and other great nations. At the same time, the NAM's focus began to shift from issues vis-à-vis the superpowers and East-West confrontation, and towards development issues involving questions regarding North-South relations. The overlap between the NAM, G-77 and UNCTAD has meant that a great degree of issues have been of mutual interest to all three organizations, resulting in close collaboration.[31]

## Conclusion

Since Prebisch's time, the aim of the Secretariat has been to be intellectually autonomous, in the sense that pressures from global actors would not and should not direct policy. It can be argued that this aspiration has not always been successful. As later chapters will demonstrate, the rise of globalization brought with it a concomitant assertion of neoliberalism that has had a profound impact upon the Secretariat's positions on economic matters—not to mention its overall influence. A key aspect of this has been the pressure to reform the Secretariat and the relocation of various UNCTAD activities. For instance, by the mid-1990s, UNCTAD's intergovernmental machinery had been radically reduced to three commissions from a previous total of more than 10. This reform process was launched at UNCTAD VIII, held at Cartagena, Colombia, in 1992 (see Chapter 5). The reform included virtually all facets of the Secretariat, such as its intergovernmental machinery, mandate and program orientations. As a result, UNCTAD holds the distinction of being the first UN body to be fully reformed through an intergovernmental agreement.

UNCTAD VIII introduced reforms in four key areas, that have impacted upon the Secretariat in a major way. These were namely, a refocus on research and policy analysis to emphasize *national* policies—an obvious step away from UNCTAD's previous focus on international and structural issues. The TDB's subsidiary bodies were directed to focus on commodity flows and trade facilitation, as well as to emphasize the role technology can play in development. And UNCTAD's mandate was broadened to conduct new research on comparative experiences with privatization. All these reforms reflected the rise of a more market-based philosophy within the global political economy and also, it can be argued, moved the Secretariat away from addressing structural issues of global inequality and underdevelopment and towards a closer agreement with the dominant mindset that reigned in the developed capitals—neoliberalism. Yet the Secretariat *has* survived and is active. Its evolution and current structure reflects the development of the organization over time although its activities and even central premises have been altered—in some ways radically—through the reform process. However, its activities, most keenly reflected in the research output and publications emanating from Geneva, means that UNCTAD's Secretariat remains central to the organization and its future direction.

# 3 Research, analysis and major publications

The research that UNCTAD has performed over the years has been seen by many as the key comparative advantage that the organization has over other bodies. It is certainly a major facet of the Secretariat's role and so naturally follows on from the previous chapter. Of note is the fact that through its research output, UNCTAD has made some significant contributions to global debates on development and the broader political economy. Obviously during the NIEO moment this was quite evident but even during the "retreat" of the organization (see Chapter 5) UNCTAD was successful in critiquing established views and challenging opinions and positions emanating from the North. For instance, as the 1980s progressed, UNCTAD was quite active in questioning the results of structural adjustment programs in the developing world. And it was UNCTAD's research on debt that arguably provided the intellectual argument later used by the Jubilee 2000 campaign. Research on commodities by the organization also continued to draw attention to the continuing decline in the terms of trade for developing nations. Other work raised concern about the nature and effect of the WTO. Indeed, UNCTAD's research—often in tandem with the UNDP's *Human Development Report*—gave incontrovertible proof that globalization and liberalization was not the willy-nilly panacea for the world's problems. The yearly *Trade and Development Report* has often acted in the same way. It can be stated that the research output of UNCTAD is indeed fundamental to the organization and a principal aspect of its work and contemporary rationale.

## UNCTAD's research in context

It would be true to say that research and analysis has always been the foundation of UNCTAD's mandate, and the work that the organization does in providing comprehensive data on a range of topics, and presenting it in a user-friendly manner is invaluable to both researchers and policy makers.[1] In conducting studies on global economic issues, particularly relating to trade, foreign direct investment and development, much of UNCTAD's intellectual contributions have resulted from close collaborations with developing country governments, who have looked to the Secretariat for new ideas and approaches. Gibbs and Ognivtsev emphasize the importance of this role in stating, "Throughout its history the UNCTAD secretariat has injected ideas and analysis into the international trade debate with the goal of constructing an international trading system more consistent with the needs and aspirations of developing countries."[2]

Former UNCTAD secretary-general Rubens Ricupero points out that the changes of recent decades, including the emergence of the WTO, and the dispersal of developing countries' positions and interests necessitated an urgent rethink of the role and future of the organization. The solution was a reinvented organization focused even more on the generation of knowledge—in Ricupero's words, "an entity grounded on knowledge and at the service of developing countries—a laboratory of innovative ideas, ethically committed to the struggle for creating more equitable conditions for the least developed as well as the excluded or marginalized countries."[3]

In carrying out its research and analysis function, UNCTAD draws on a combination of in-house expertise, as well as a network of academics and policy makers which it has built up over the years. These external experts fulfill a dual role in that not only do they contribute to the organization's meetings and publications, but they also participate in a peer review process that ensures that outputs are of a high quality. As Fredriksson[4] notes, one only needs to look at the acknowledgments at the beginning of each *WIR* to realize the involvement of academics, officials from central banks, investment promotion agencies and representatives of nongovernmental organizations (NGOs) in each publication. In addition, there has been a realization that, besides working directly with governments, the involvement of members of civil society (including universities, NGOs and the press) could be of great assistance in influencing the positions of governments. The rationale is that these entities are better able to effect a change in perception in their national governments than pressure by developing countries under the auspices of UNCTAD.

The organization has, however, also come under fire regarding the external sources providing intellectual advice to the organization. There have been suggestions that UNCTAD relies to a large degree on inputs from researchers based in the developed world and that it should, instead, consult more widely with experts based at research institutions in the developing world.[5] This criticism is based on the underlying assumption that "African solutions to African problems" are preferable to "European solutions to African problems." Part of it stems from the experiences of the developing world of the prescriptive policies (such as the structural adjustment policies of the 1980s) enforced by northern international financial institutions such as the IMF and the World Bank, as well as donor governments. There is also the related issue of the neo-imperialist nature of knowledge from the north, and the (ir)relevance of such knowledge to the realities and challenges of the developing world. In pursuing its research work, UNCTAD therefore needs to take heed of the perception that the answers to the problems experienced by the developing world can (only) be found in the developed world.

According to former UNCTAD secretary-general Rubens Ricupero,[6] it is possible to identify three major trends in the Secretariat's analytical and research work. The first has been mainly of an information-gathering and statistics-generating nature, with the Secretariat doing comprehensive studies on the state of the global economy, the nature and effects of the processes of globalization and liberalization, and the changing role of TNCs and global FDI flows. A large part of this work entails continuous data-collection work, in cooperation with national data-collecting agencies.

More important than simply providing raw data and statistical tools has been UNCTAD's analytical role, which has resulted in it becoming a breeding ground for new ideas and approaches to trade and development. Throughout its history, the UNCTAD Secretariat has provided the intellectual leadership on trade issues. Gibbs and Ognivtsev[7] highlight some of the milestones, including the recognition of changes in the international trading system in the 1980s, and the effects on developing countries. The Secretariat was also the first to explore the relationship between development and trade in services. More recently, the Secretariat has led the way in addressing the concerns of developing countries relating to the process of accession to the WTO.

In this way, the organization has been at the forefront of dealing with new and emerging developments and trends in the global economy, especially as they relate to the developing world. It has relentlessly sought to find new ways of looking at the development dilemma, and proposing strategies by which existing economic activity could be integrated into the promotion of not only economic growth but also development. As a result, the organization's work has moved well beyond focusing on trade and has expanded to include almost all areas related to the world economy, ranging from shipping to the environment and tourism. The practical import of UNCTAD's research work can be seen in the reliance of many developing countries on UNCTAD's research and analysis in determining their trade, investment, development and other policies.

The second trend has been of a more critical nature, involving an analysis and critique of the Washington Consensus, and the approach to development that it has advocated. The Secretariat's role has been more than just a critical one—it has also made recommendations regarding alternative approaches to development, favoring a more pluralistic approach that takes into account national and regional differences.

The final focus of the Secretariat's work has involved highlighting the asymmetries and inequalities inherent in the global trading system. The existence of these imbalances underpins the work of the entire organization—everything it does is geared towards addressing these global inequities and proposing measures to help level the global trading playing field, with UNCTAD acting as an important forum for negotiations in the North-South dialogue. On the basis of this contribution, UNCTAD has received much praise. A recent review of the organization by the South Centre states, "If there is today a greater transparency in the world economic system, it is in no small measure due to the relentless manner in which UNCTAD, particularly in its initial years, went about exposing the unfairness of the system."[8]

The organization has also gone beyond simply exposing these asymmetries to proposing strategies to address and rectify them, and calling for a rethinking of existing approaches to trade and development. Persuading developed countries that correcting the asymmetries of the current global system would be to the benefit of all as it would ultimately lead to a more stable world economy, has been one of UNCTAD's ongoing challenges.

Finally, it is important to note that the organization's research work is not only an end in itself, but has been instrumental in informing technical assistance work in the field. It is impossible to develop and implement policies in particular areas without access to the necessary data and statistics. There has therefore always been a close association between UNCTAD's research and analysis, on the one hand, and advisory and assistance efforts on the other. Suggestions have, however, been made that this is an area where there is considerable scope for improvement due to the fact that the linkages between UNCTAD's analytical and operational activities are not always optimal.[9]

UNCTAD disseminates its research and analysis through its flagship publications, as well as through occasional publications and databases. An overview of its major publications follows.[10]

## *Trade and Development Report (TDR)*[11]

Ever since it was first published in 1981, UNCTAD's annual *Trade and Development Report* has established itself as one of the most authoritative sources of data and analysis on current global economic performance, trade, finance, debt, macroeconomic policies and poverty. Its objective is to identify policies that facilitate development and assist developing countries to integrate into the world economy. In addition, every year the *TDR* focuses on a particular issue related to development within the context of globalization. Due to the depth and quality of analysis found in the report, it is also highly rated as a prescriptive document, proposing new trading and development strategies.

The *TDR* also constitutes one of the major intellectual contributions of the organization to understanding developments in the international trade, monetary and financial systems. The *TDR*s of the early 1980s, for example, grappled with what was regarded as the need for a new development discourse, given the changing global environment and increasing interdependence between all states, rich and poor. Part of this work entailed conceptualizing the process of globalization in all its various facets. Later reports (e.g. *TDR 1996*[12]) conducted in-depth analyses of globalization, taking a critical look at its costs, and asking probing questions about the potential benefit to the lives of the world's poor. The reports have also done exploratory studies on other important developments in the world economy—such as China's accession to the WTO—and what the implications are for developing countries. Similarly, *TDR*s in the mid-1990s (in particular *TDR 1994,*[13] *TDR 1996* and *TDR 1997*[14]) explored the potential for the East-Asian economic success story to be replicated elsewhere in the developing world. Following the collapse of the East-Asian economies, the *TDR*s also played an important role in the intellectual clarification regarding the causes and effects of financial crises, and in providing proposals for dealing with such crises.

The reports have therefore addressed a number of issues pertinent to the developing world, pointing out the structural impediments they face in trying to achieve economic growth and development. The 2002 *TDR,*[15] for example, explored the apparent paradox that, while developing countries are trading more, they are earning comparatively less. Throughout, the argument has been that integration into the global trading system is not a sufficient condition for development. Similarly, the *TDR*s continue to question the assumption that growth in exports and FDI will lead to income gains, in other words that greater openness to international trade and finance will automatically result in increased growth and development.

Over the years, the *TDR* has established itself not only as an authoritative voice on global economic issues, but has also become known for the way in which it challenges conventional ways of thinking about development. This has resulted in economic forecasting which differs quite significantly from that found in other sources. In line with the organization's role as an intellectual watchdog, successive *TDR*s have advanced comprehensive critical assessments of structural adjustment and Washington Consensus policies.

The focus of the reports remains the high level of global trade imbalances, and on finding ways to improve this state of affairs. In exposing the root causes, the reports have pointed to the role of developments in the industrialized states, and the compounding effects of the international monetary and financial systems have also been highlighted.

The most recent issues (*TDR 2005*[16] and *TDR 2006*[17]) have found that, despite some positive effects of world economic expansion, global imbalances continue to pose a risk to developing countries. While the economic growth of China and India has benefited other developing countries through rising commodity prices, a consequence of these two countries' rising consumption of natural resources, the reports warn that these effects may be short-lived. In addition, progress towards growth and development remains slow in many parts of the world, particularly sub-Saharan Africa. In working towards the achievement of the Millennium Development Goals (MDGs), in particular the global partnership for development, the conclusion is that the goals cannot be reached without reforming the global economic governance system.

## *World Investment Report* (*WIR*)[18]

Another one of the organization's flagship publications, this report is a major source of information on global FDI trends as well as the activities of TNCs.[19] In addition to providing information on worldwide trends, each year's report also conducts an in-depth analysis of one selected topic related to FDI and development. The first two *WIR*s (1991 and 1992) were published by the United Nations Center on TNCs (UNCTC), with UNCTAD assuming responsibility for their publication in 1993, when the center was closed down and its activities transferred to Geneva.

The reports have been instrumental in ensuring that the impacts of FDI and TNCs are accorded a more prominent role in international economic relations. They have also played a major part in the conceptual development of these phenomena. *WIR 1991*,[20] for example, explored the role that TNCs play in promoting economic growth and regional economic development, while *WIR 1993*[21] provided an overview of the evolving strategies and organizational structures of TNCs, including an empirical documentation of their integrated international production systems. Considerable research has also been done on the geography of FDI, with each *WIR* providing an overview and analysis of global and regional trends in FDI flows. According to John H. Dunning, the long-standing Senior Adviser to the *WIR* team, the impact of the *WIR*s in this regard cannot be underestimated. He notes how "[s]uccessive *WIR*s have helped governments, in a way no other publication has done, to know about TNCs—their nature, strategies and likely impact; and to guide them in their information gathering, policy formulation, institution building, and implementation devices."[22]

The reports have also contributed significantly to shaping the debate around FDI and development, and the apparent tension between the indisputable potential benefits of FDI versus, on the other hand, its negative effects. Making this issue its main focus, *WIR 1999: FDI and the Challenge of Development*[23] was the culmination of what had been the underlying thread through all of the *WIR*s in the 1990s. As has been mentioned earlier in the book, the attitude towards FDI and TNCs within UNCTAD gradually changed from one of skepticism and criticism towards one of increasing recognition of the benefits of FDI to promoting development. Much of the *WIR*'s work has therefore involved analyzing the determinants of FDI, and developing policies aimed at attracting investment. The *WIR 1998*,[24] for example, found that there had been a decline in traditional FDI determinants (such as natural resources and cheap labor). Subsequently, its recommendation to developing country governments was to develop what were identified to be the new FDI determinants—including access to technology and regional markets, and local skills. Similarly, *WIR 2000*[25] explored the different modes of entry of TNCs, arguing that understanding of these processes would enable governments to develop policies aimed at attracting certain types of FDI that would be beneficial to development. Approaching the challenge of attracting investment from the bottom up, the *WIR 2005*[26] identified particular deficiencies of countries not able to attract investment. Such studies are crucial in a time when, despite governments' push for liberalization of FDI and the introduction of a large number of international investment agreements (IIAs), the majority of developing countries have experienced a decline in investment since the turn of the millennium.

As is the case with the *Trade and Development Report*, the prescriptive component is an important one, with the reports making policy recommendations relating to the role that FDI can play as a growth engine for development. *WIR 2001*[27] and *WIR 2002,*[28] for example, formulated policies aimed at achieving linkages between FDI and domestic enterprises, and export promotion involving foreign affiliates. This was based on the finding that links between local companies in the developing world and TNCs are crucial to reaping the benefits of FDI. The reports have consistently emphasized the important role that government policies can play in ensuring that FDI flows have a positive impact on national economies. They have also been prescriptive in outlining the social responsibility of TNCs, with *WIR 1999* and *WIR 2003*[29] exploring the question whether TNCs have an obligation to contribute directly to development in the countries in which they invest.

An indication of the interest in this annual publication can be found in the *DITE's 2005 Activities Report*, which states that previous *WIR*s were downloaded two million times during 2005, while the 2005 report was downloaded more than 600,000 times within the first three months of publication.[30] However, despite much praise for UNCTAD's work in this field, there have also been some critical voices calling for the organization's research and analysis on FDI and TNCs, especially as presented in the *WIR*, to be more independent and critical of the development impact of FDI.[31]

## *Investment Policy Reviews* (*IPR*s)[32]

An extension of the work done by the *WIR*s, the *IPR*s, which were first launched at UNCTAD IX in 1996, are funded by the United Nations Development Program (UNDP) and donor governments. Initiated at the request of individual governments, the reviews are done in close collaboration with national governments, and provide in-depth analyses of a country's comparative advantages, as well as recommendations for improvements.

While the *WIR* aims at providing an overview of global investment trends, these reviews fulfill a dual role. They are aimed, on the one hand, at assisting developing and transition country governments to improve their investment context and policies, and also serve as a forum for the exchange of best practices. On the other hand, they also provide other governments and the private sector with up-to-date information about the investment climate of particular countries. Assistance to individual countries goes beyond recommendations on improving the investment climate; proposals are also given with regard to reaping greater developmental benefits from FDI.

It is also important to note that *IPRs* are more than just reports, and are instead treated as a process involving considerable follow-up activities and assistance to governments.

## *Least Developed Countries Report (LDCR)*[33]

These reports, which were previously published annually but became biennial in 2000, are the UN's most comprehensive source of socio-economic data and analysis of the world's poorest countries. In addition, they identify major challenges and international support measures concerning these countries, and focus on ways in which international trade can be a catalyst for development and poverty alleviation. The reports, which are intended for a broad readership of governments, policy makers, researchers and all those involved with LDCs development policies, each contain a statistical annex, which provides basic data on the LDCs. In addition, each report focuses on a particular issue of concern to these countries, with recent ones placing a particular spotlight on targets identified in the *Action Plan for the LDCs* and the Millennium Development Goals.

A significant stumbling block for researchers compiling the *LDCR*s has been the lack of available data in LDCs. As Younger[34] points out in his review of the 2002 report, national household surveys are conducted very irregularly in LDCs, which makes cross-country comparisons and time series exceptionally challenging. The report has however attempted to address some of these shortcomings in developing new methods—a case in point was the *LDCR 2002*[35] which presented a new method of calculating poverty rates across time and across different countries.

Analyzing international poverty has been a central theme throughout the reports, with much criticism directed at international efforts to alleviate poverty in the poorest nations. An initial assessment of the Poverty Reduction Strategy Paper (PRSP)[36] approach undertaken in the *LDCR 2000*[37] was built upon in the *LDCR 2002*, which argued that structural adjustment will not lead to economic growth, and eventually poverty reduction. As part of its critique of the PRSP approach, the report also claimed that LDCs were caught in an international poverty trap, which was being exacerbated by the international trade and financial systems and the processes of globalization. It went on to propose the adoption of alternative, development-oriented poverty reduction strategies. The relationship between poverty and trade was again taken up in the *LDCR 2004,*[38] which found that, although trade has the potential to act as a major force in poverty reduction, this is not happening in practice. It goes on to explore some of the reasons—ranging from weak trade performance by LDCs through conflict to a tendency towards exclusionary rather than socially equitable trade-induced economic growth. The fact that, despite efforts by LDCs to liberalize their economies, and privileged market access, the result has not been a reduction of poverty, was also highlighted.

Another issue that has remained a focal point of the reports since the 1980s has been the importance of national institutional capacity building, and the improvement of productive capacities in the LDCs. The most recent (*LDCR 2006*[39]) issue again argues that the development of domestic productive capacities is key to sustainable economic growth and poverty reduction. Whilst aimed at a wide audience, many of the proposals made in the reports have thus targeted policy makers in LDCs, based on the assumption that national development strategies are crucial to improving the trade-poverty relationship.

The role that international support mechanisms can play in promoting development and reducing poverty in the LDCs has, however, not been overlooked. In the context of dropping levels of official development assistance (ODA), the *LDCR 1999*[40] and *LDCR 2000* emphasized the importance of ODA and debt relief, highlighting the fact that development prospects in most LDCs depend critically on external aid. In addition, reform of the multilateral trading system has been a recurrent theme, with calls for fundamental changes going beyond the provision of preferential access to LDCs.

The proposals made in the *LDCR 2004* summarize UNCTAD's multi-faceted approach to addressing the challenges of development and poverty reduction in the LDCs. The report identified national and international policies that can make trade a more effective mechanism for poverty reduction in these countries, calling for action on three fronts: developing national strategies that combine trade and development concerns with the aim of reducing poverty; increasing international financial and technical assistance to improve domestic production and trade capacities; and promoting a more favorable international trade regime.

## *Review of Maritime Transport*[41]

First published in 1968, this annual publication provides comprehensive and up-to-date information on maritime services. Reporting on the worldwide evolution of shipping, ports and multimodal transport, its main purpose is to monitor trends in world maritime transport and to provide relevant statistical data. It also identifies trends in seaborne trade and analyzes the performance of maritime activities. Emphasis is given to the development of the merchant marines in developing countries as compared with other groups of countries, and to the relationship between development of global trade and activities of overall maritime transport.

Trade facilitation in general is an important area explored by the reviews, in light of the realization that countries with insufficient transport facilities are not in a good position to attract trade. In addition, a lack of adequate transport and logistics systems also prevents the development of increased production and export capacity. Issues such as the impact of customs procedures and the lengthy waiting time at borders are also addressed, especially as they affect the competitiveness of developing countries. Each review includes a special chapter featuring developments in a particular region of the developing world, with *RMT 2005*[42] featuring Latin America and the Caribbean, *RMT 2004*[43] Asia, and *RMT 2003*[44] sub-Saharan Africa.

The publication is aimed at Ministries of Transport, intergovernmental organizations dealing with trade facilitation, port authorities, academia and other trade and transportation research institutions, exporters/importers and related organizations and transport operators mainly, but not exclusively, in developing countries. The review has been one of UNCTAD's main contributions to shipping, and has provided valuable information on the shipping industry to assist developing country delegations in their trade negotiations. In particular, it provides a comprehensive database on supply and demand in world shipping.

## *Handbook of Statistics* and statistical online databases

The handbook contains a comprehensive collection of basic indicators of trade, development and investment, such as per capita GDP and growth rates for individual countries and for economic and trade groupings. Statistical interpretation and analysis is facilitated through the use of rank orderings, growth rates and other special calculations.[45] The statistics are based on existing national and international data sources, while some of the series represent UNCTAD Secretariat estimates.

Topics covered by the handbook include indices of trade and commodity prices, the structure of international trade by region and by product, development indicators, international financial statistics, and international trade in services statistics. The statistics are used in analyzing global trade and FDI, and also for making sense of the economic trends of developing countries over the past decades in the context of globalization. The handbook is available as a printed edition, in CD-ROM format, and online, with the latter providing time series of economic data and development indicators which allow comparative research and analyses of trends in the global economy over time.

In order to facilitate accessibility, data is increasingly being made available online (UNCTAD website), and a number of analytical and statistical tools have been developed, focusing specifically on measuring globalization and its implications for developing countries. One such tool is the Commodity Price Statistics On-Line Database, which provides monthly indices and monthly averages of daily and weekly commodity prices since 1960, and provides a valuable service to producers, government officials and researchers alike. Another is the UNCTAD TRAINS (Trade Analysis and Information System), a comprehensive computerized database system providing online access to information about trade flows and trade control measures for over 130 countries. In addition, it also provides country notes of trade regimes for some 40 developing countries, describing market access conditions according to the UNCTAD Coding System of Trade Control Measures. It is another example of how UNCTAD's research informs the technical assistance provided by the organization, making available information that can be used by developing countries in preparing for multilateral trade negotiations and to get the know-how enabling them to integrate into the global economy. Finally, the FDI database presents inflows, outflows, inward stocks and outward stocks of foreign direct investment for 196 reporting economies in an interactive format.

## Conclusion

As this chapter has demonstrated, research and analysis remain one of UNCTAD's major functions. However, despite the contributions the organization has made through its analytical work, there have clearly also been areas where it has been found lacking.

One such instance is the contention that UNCTAD's analysis focuses only on inequalities between developed and developing nations, to the exclusion of growing inequalities within these countries. By employing such a simplistic North-South model of the world, asymmetries cutting across this divide are overlooked. The call is thus for UNCTAD to not only concern itself with the fate of those in the developing world, but the poor and marginalized everywhere.[46] Incorporating such a suggestion would however significantly broaden the organization's mandate and does pose the danger of diluting its focus.

Another point on which UNCTAD has been criticized is that although there has been much praise for the critical and independent nature of analysis in publications like the *Trade and Development Report*, this level of analysis is not consistent throughout the organization's work. There have been calls by some representatives of civil society that UNCTAD's work on FDI and TNCs, especially as found in the *World Investment Report*, should, for example, be more critical of the development impact of FDI. Relatedly, there have also been calls for UNCTAD's analysis to incorporate a wider range of alternative approaches—such as human rights and feminism.[47] In rejecting the mainstream neoliberal approach to development, it is easy to fall into the trap of simply blindly adopting a different model, without consideration of the possible contributions that peripheral approaches could make to understanding some of the issues dealt with.

Finally, on a more practical level, the dissemination of the research and analysis produced by UNCTAD, an area in which the organization excelled during its early years, has been identified as another challenge. It is felt that while a select audience (mostly the academic community and NGOs) are aware of UNCTAD's work more effort needs to go into disseminating this information to developing country governments.[48]

In conclusion, UNCTAD's research and analysis has undoubtedly made a valuable intellectual contribution not only to the host of trade and development issues facing the developing world, but also to promoting a better understanding of the structure and workings of the world economy in general. Importantly, UNCTAD has been instrumental in exposing the negative effects of processes like globalization, and has recommended strategies for dealing with these impacts. In light of the ever-changing nature of the international system, new developments in international trade, and the restructuring of the UN, the organization will continuously have to reposition itself to justify its relevance.

In its appraisal of the current status of UNCTAD, the South Centre highlights the importance of an integrated approach to analysis, in which UNCTAD could take the lead. According to a recent report,[49] one of UNCTAD's defining features during the first few decades of its existence was the holistic view it took of global economic issues, within an integrated conceptual framework. The analysis that flowed from this then became the basis of intergovernmental deliberations. It proceeds to lament that such an integrated analysis of international development is currently lacking in the UN system, and calls for UNCTAD to become the institutional center for a renewed integrated approach. Suggestions are made as to the topics that are currently analyzed by different UN agencies in isolation from one another, which could be better addressed together. These include the processes and impacts of globalization, environmental challenges, management of international goods, and inequities in the global trading and financial systems. Continuing its tradition of providing comprehensive research and alternative analysis of global economic trends, and doing so in an integrated way, seems to be one area in which UNCTAD can continue to make a valuable contribution. In fact, in the context of debates around the organization's future, this would seem to be *the* crucial area where it has a comparative advantage over rival institutions.

# 4 "Golden years," 1960s–1970s

The early years of UNCTAD's existence can be seen to be the heydays of the organization. It was during this period, roughly from the foundation of the body until the early 1980s, that UNCTAD emerged as a vigorous champion of the developing world and one that was relatively successful in advancing some quite important demands within multilateral fora. Indeed, the promotion of the New International Economic Order, although ultimately failing, staked out much of the intellectual debate within the global political economy throughout the 1970s. Thus an account of the history of UNCTAD during this period allows the reader to gain an insight into not only the past activities of the organization, but also how and why the heady days of the NIEO and UNCTAD as a "vanguard" body, were only momentary. This is important if one wishes to understand UNCTAD's current status and role.

"UNCTAD" at first referred to the Conference that took place in 1964 in Geneva. But as detailed earlier, the UN General Assembly later sanctioned UNCTAD to become a permanent organization, with periodic ministerial conferences held every three or four years. The name UNCTAD is thus somewhat of a misnomer and has caused confusion in the past as it is not simply a conference but is a permanent body. Having said that, the regular ministerial conferences, which make up the session of UNCTAD, remain the organization's premier policy-making site, creating the body's key policies and establishing the parameters of UNCTAD's work programs before the next Conference. Thus the Ministerial Conference is important in shaping the work and direction of UNCTAD and as a result, the Ministerial Conferences have historically been the site of major contestations about the organization's shape and policy preferences. Indeed, the Ministerial Conferences have been important markers in the process of North-South dialogue and debate vis-à-vis trade and development. The ideological struggles and changes that have taken place globally can in fact be reflected in the shape and character of the Ministerial Conferences of the past and present.

In short, the first five Conferences might be said to have been based on ideas underpinned by Dependency Theory and in a broader milieu that was *relatively* sympathetic to both Southern claims and the general nature of the North-South debate. These five Conferences have been viewed as the highlight of UNCTAD's existence in some quarters, and certainly stake out what might be seen as the "golden age" of the organization.

## Intellectual background to UNCTAD I-III

Dependency Theory emerged from Latin America and directly engaged the Modernization School in a robust fashion, particularly pointing out the ahistorical weakness of the Modernization Theory's broad model. It was particularly influential within UNCTAD during the 1970s. The weakness of Modernization Theory was that it posited that all societies started from a comparative stage of development (the initial "stage of growth") and hence would—or could—follow comparable paths to modernization. This path however pictured the North's model (which was diffuse and varied anyway) as the norm against which all "progress" should be evaluated. Such an approach of course immediately granted a form of legitimizing capitalist growth models as the path to modernization, while delegitimizing non-capitalist models, an actuality that fitted perfectly with what was after all, a "non-Communist manifesto." In addition, later studies showed that societies in the South, even when they took on board technologies from the North, did not necessarily abandon their "primitive" social formations and in fact in many cases actually had their own non-capitalist cultures strengthened.[1]

In reaction, the *dependencistas* argued that the North and the South were different precisely because of their different histories. This was a simple point to make but a necessary one in the light of the modernizers' tendency to the collapsing of past historical trajectories. In addition, it was asserted that the South's relationship to the North was historically contingent and that its current status of impoverishment and dependence was comparatively recent: the South had not always been poor. Indeed, Dependency Theory clearly showed that the roots of the South's impoverishment lay in the process by which it had been integrated into the capitalist world economy during the colonial period.[2] Colonialism had integrated the South, but at a subordinate position in the emerging global division of labor, playing itself out in the way in which the South came to supply primary goods to the North: a highly problematic scenario for the South with the instability of markets for primary commodities acting as a sword of Damocles over their future development. The concomitant importing of processed goods from the developed world presented equally difficult problems—the choice being either a continual run on foreign exchange reserves or an expensive import substitution program.

In the process of forcibly integrating the South into the capitalist world economy, already-existing local industries situated in the South were consciously and deliberately swept aside by an emergent Northern bourgeoisie.[3] The case of India's cotton industry is an oft-cited but revealing example. In short, the colonization process resulted in the South's economies being oriented more toward the needs of Northern capital than the requirements of the local. This was the quintessential definition of dependency, although Dependency Theory itself was divided into various schools: orthodox Dependency Theory;[4] World Systems;[5] and "unorthodox" Dependency Theory.[6]

Rather than picture an ahistorical "level playing field" whereby each social formation needed to simply go through the ideal-type stages of growth, the *dependencistas* rather asserted that the North had an advantage from the start in that they never had to—at least in modern times—experience colonial rule nor, attempt to integrate themselves into a global economy already replete with richer and more powerful competitors. Comparing then the experiences of North and South, certainly at the early stages of development, was a futile exercise as far as Dependency Theory was concerned.

Dependency Theory also pointed out that the relationships of dependency crafted during the Age of Expansionism by the colonial powers, were continued long after "official" rule by the colonizers was over. This "neocolonialism" was recognized early on even by Southern elites—Nkrumah's analysis being a famous example.[7] Only by recognizing this can a true appreciation of North-South relations be realized. This asserted that the main obstacles to real autonomous development were not internal, but were rather external in origin and contingently bound up with the historical experiences of the spread of international capitalism.[8] This then was Dependency Theory's approach to North-South relations, an approach that rapidly gained ground in the thinking of many elites in the South as a means to explain the relative failure of the post-colonial states to develop according to Modernization Theory's remits. Though Dependency Theory was in fact a broad church, its essential premise was the same, and was highly influential, bringing about what Cox and Jacobson called "a shift in the dominant ideology ... to developmentalism."[9] How this played out in the politics of North-South relations and its influence on Southern thinking vis-à-vis the international political economy is what we shall turn to next.

## North-South relations and the confrontational moment

The South's development post-1945 and the early years of UNCTAD were in essence a micro-process within a broader macro-process. This broader milieu was the post-war economic-political settlement, the "embedded liberalism" of the Bretton Woods Institutions (BWI) and its sister groups, namely the World Bank, the International Monetary Fund (IMF), and the General Agreement on Tariffs and Trade (GATT)—now the World Trade Organization (WTO).[10] This was in essence a post-war "Golden Age" of relative economic and political stability. Under the aegis of the BWI, "mixed economies" and a liberalizing international economy became central to this arrangement. This settlement stimulated the development of economic-political agents: externally oriented transnational corporations, national (inwardly-looking) monopolistic/oligopolistic corporations, and state administrations.[11] These agents created in both the North and, to a lesser degree the South, "triple alliances" which overlooked the economic and political evolution of both. This occurred at a historic juncture when the newly independent nations of the South were flexing their muscles and there was a heady optimism regarding the maneuverability of the developing world vis-à-vis the North. Indeed, some writers, asserting that dependent relations constructed during the colonial period precluded development within the wider world economy, advocated an autocentric "de-linking" from the capitalist world economy.[12] This did not imply an autarkic utopia, but rather a development strategy that emphasized domestic requirements over excessive reliance on external demand. Such impulses have not died, and retain an attraction to a number of scholars disillusioned with the marginalizing processes at work alongside a deepening globalization.[13]

This then was a moment when the *possibility* of challenging global norms regarding trade and development was potentially realizable, and when—as it became ever more apparent that Modernization Theory was deeply problematic—there *were* alternatives. Both UNCTAD's and the Non-Aligned Movement's (NAM) formation—but in particular UNCTAD's—reflected not only the growth in membership in the United Nations (UN) of states of the South, but also a steady disillusionment with an ever-apparent unequal world order.[14] This was particularly so as this was an order in which the new states had had no hand in forming. Consequently, "the crystallization of developing countries into a single bloc for the purpose of international economic negotiations represented a direct challenge to industrialized countries."[15] And Dependency Theory provided an intellectual framework through which critics of the ongoing world order made sense of the global political economy. Such positions more and more dominated debate within UNCTAD.

Yet there were attempts to find a middle ground between the North and the South that sought to avoid the logical conclusions associated with *dependencia* and the necessary restructuring of world trade.[16] As a result, the declarations emanating from these conferences were in the main moderate and, arguably, compromised. Furthermore, and this was to become increasingly problematic, while UNCTAD was pursuing the NIEO, it was also enthusiastically behind developing countries' governments and their claimed fight for development and the reduction of poverty. This was a position that was generally uncritical of these governments, despite the fact that many of them were actually anti-developmental in nature and mired in corruption and despotism. Also, it took at face value their stated commitments to the NIEO, ignoring that in fact:

> Third World elites were not the passive victims of the US liquidation of the development project. At least some fractions of such elites [i.e., the externally oriented] were among the strongest supporters of the new Washington Consensus through which the liquidation was accomplished. To the extent that this has been the case, Third World elites have been among the social forces that have promoted the liberalization of trade and capital movements.[17]

This is because state elites, particularly in countries more or less integrated into the global economy, believe that liberalization is the way to proceed: "Core interests have supported neoliberalism not only for material gain but also because there has been a genuine belief that it will lead to development. For peripheral interests . . . consent has been given with conviction that participation in the global marketplace will benefit them."[18] But we are jumping ahead of ourselves.

## The UNCTAD early years

After hard and consistent lobbying within UNCTAD, the developing world was exempted from the requirement to reciprocate in its trade with the North—a tacit recognition of the structural inequalities that the developing world suffered from and a reflection of the broadly *dependencista* ethos then current amongst those multilateral bodies ostensibly dealing with the South's problems. This engagement with GATT was based upon the knowledge that an alternative economic system in the East provided the developing world with a measure of autonomy and political space, and took a fair degree of pressure off many Southern elites that would otherwise have been applied by the developed world.[19]

The GSP has proven to be an achievement of UNCTAD as many developing countries have benefited from trade preferences for their exports to developed countries. However, the benefits have not been as beneficial as they might have been, given the North's intransigence in allowing exemption for products of particular interest for developing economies. For instance, exports of products such as textiles, shoes and clothing have been met with exemptions from the GSP and also constraints on their importation into developed nations. Furthermore, UNCTAD's pronouncements suffered a rather cynical fate. Richard Gardner, part of the American delegation to UNCTAD I, went to Paris to seek support for the position that UNCTAD should become a specialized agency rather than remaining part of the UN Secretariat. As he remembers,

> I sat with the head of Quai d'Orsay's international organization directorate . . . He said "Monsieur Gardner, we don't want any special voting. We would prefer they [i.e., the developing world] vote [on] anything they want in the normal way and then we can ignore it . . . Leave everything as it is."[20]

The third ministerial conference, UNCTAD III, met in Santiago, Chile, in 1972. A draft Charter of the Economic Rights and Duties of States was proposed by Mexico and was debated by an UNCTAD Working Group, which in 1974 presented the draft Charter to the UN General Assembly. This Charter was then adopted in December 1974 as Resolution 3281 (XXIX) of the General Assembly. It has been described as "the most uncompromisingly absolutist assertion of the primacy of sovereignty to have been produced in the modern era."[21] Indeed, Article 10 states:

> All States are juridically equal and, as equal members of the international community, have the right to participate fully and effectively in the international decision-making process in the

> solution of world economic, financial and monetary problems, inter alia, through the appropriate international organizations in accordance with their existing and evolving rules, and to share equitably in the benefits resulting there from.

It should be pointed out that the Charter was part and parcel of the South's push for a NIEO noted above, and staked out a new development within UNCTAD from advancing improvement of the ongoing trading and economic system (the goals of both UNCTAD I and II) to the founding of a new global order aimed at a restructuring of the world in favor of the developing countries. Indeed, UNCTAD's Charter followed on from the Sixth Special Session of the UN in May 1974 where, under the NAM's then leader (Algeria's Honari Boumedienne), the South deployed NAM and G-77 texts in successfully pushing for a comprehensive normative declaration detailing the aspirations of the developing world's elites. Murphy asserted that:

> [F]or the first time the General Assembly approved a massive resolution covering all of the economic issues the Third World had raised since the Second World War. The resolution touched on sovereignty over natural resources, improving terms of trade through international regulation of trade based on equitable treatment, reforming the global monetary system to include an aid component, expanding concessionary multilateral aid, providing debt relief, controlling TNCs, promoting international support for industrialization, and reforming the United Nations system to give Third World governments greater control over international economic decisions.[22]

Much of this rhetoric was derivative of Southern elites' perceptions of their own domestic interests within the context of the breakdown of the Bretton Woods system and the maneuverings of the OPEC states. With the end of the regulatory framework of the Bretton Woods arrangements, negotiations regarding the future architecture to replace such a system seemed logical to many Southern elites. In short, they took the opportunities afforded by the evolving politics to generate leadership positions for themselves, thereby bolstering their own standing at the domestic level. The key principles around both the Charter and more broadly the NIEO were based on a dirigiste understanding of the role of the state in development and a rejection of the "free market" as a vehicle for the same, arguing that it exacerbated inequalities within and between states. In addition, the principle of non-reciprocity in commercial trading relations between the North and the South was taken as a given by the Charter and by the advocates of the NIEO.

UNCTAD III was probably the highpoint for those advocates of a NIEO and a "fairer" world order.[23] Indeed "Third World [elites emerged] claiming a role in international crisis management that only the United States was trying hard to ignore."[24] A proposal by Brazil to organize a Charter for a proposed International Trade and Development Organization, which was aimed at merging UNCTAD and the GATT, was rejected after debate in the TDB.[25]

That UNCTAD III was the highpoint of the new ideas being advanced by the South was proven by the relatively sterile debates that surrounded UNCTAD IV in Nairobi, 1976 and UNCTAD V in Manila, 1979.[26] Somewhat ironically, given the discourse that was to sweep UNCTAD and all other multilateral organizations in the 1980s, the subject of structural adjustment was advanced. However, this was structural adjustment *in the North*, to facilitate the comparative advantages that were deemed to benefit developing countries. Structural adjustment in the developed world was promoted (albeit very temporarily) as a means to make possible greater increases in exports from the South. The idea of structural adjustment was linked to the fear that protectionism was still holding sway in the developed economies, in spite of the conclusion of the Tokyo Round of multilateral trade negotiations in 1979.

However, the major capitalist powers adopted policies of "selective intervention and subsidy in support of particular sectors, enterprises or regions within their own domestic economy."[27] Indeed, the action by many Western administrations—selective liberalization—allowed the state elites to lessen the impact of tariff cuts and permitted them to protect politically sensitive parts of their national economies. Not only would this protect the specific elites situated at the head of such "sensitive" (and usually strategically important) industries but it also allowed the national leadership to posture a protective stance towards those labor constituencies it was shielding.

In addition, UNCTAD's schema for establishing a set level for commodity prices fair to both exporters and importers and for improving the competitiveness of commodities as well as assisting primary product exporters to diversify their profile became what Biel called the NIEO's "make-or-break issue."[28] UNCTAD IV started to try and negotiate what became known as the Integrated Program of Commodities (IPC):

> Just as GSP had become the symbol of the New Delhi UNCTAD II in 1968, commodity schemes were the symbol of the early 1970s and indeed at the Nairobi UNCTAD IV in 1976 when the negotiations on the Integrated Program for Commodities were agreed upon.[29]

The broad context behind this was that by the time of Nairobi commodity prices had collapsed.[30] The IPC sought agreements for 18 specific commodities with the key aim being stabilization of prices at a level remunerative to the producers and equitable to the consumers.[31] A Common Fund would be established that would link individual international commodity agreements (ICAs), thus compensating short-term weaknesses of any one agreement through the relative strength of others.[32] However, there was a failure to agree on supporting any commodity other than rubber and this tardy response to negotiating details for individual commodities was mirrored by the long delay in establishing the Common Fund (see below).[33] This can be directly related to the North's reduced dependence (and hence vulnerability) on commodity power, excepting oil.

Indeed, the North sidetracked and delayed the whole IPC process. It was only in 1980 that the basic Article of Agreement was adopted, with an agreed fund to finance the Program, though its ratification was consistently put off. In what were to become familiar tactics within UNCTAD as the 1980s progressed, the North effectively blocked initiatives by simple inertia and it was only in 1989 that the fund actually came into existence. This reflected what Williams characterized as "Maximum demand from the G-77 tended to induce minimal response from Group B."[34]

Furthermore, the failure of the South to take advantage of the oil crises as a means to advance the NIEO fell right into the hands of the Northern elites, determined to maintain their privileges at all costs. Indeed, OPEC's failure to push home any advantage accrued by the crisis surrounding the oil hike was a major strategic error. As Augelli and Murphy point out,

> OPEC members did not use their resources as part of a complete strategy for consolidating power throughout the world economy. Rather than selectively and judiciously investing their wealth in ways that would bind new allies to [a counterhegemonic] bloc, most of the OPEC members relied upon private institutions that shared the core interests of the old historical bloc, international banks.[35]

This failure to work out a coherent strategy to construct an alternative order and the OPEC members' usage of capitalist banking institutions was to result in a fatal weakening of the South's bargaining position vis-à-vis the North and to radically undermine South solidarity; and with the recycling of petro-dollars and concomitant reckless adventurist lending practices of the North's bankers in the late 1970s to early 1980s led to the catastrophic debt crisis and the "lost decade." As Fidel Castro remarked, "OPEC policies, far from pioneering reformed North-South relations ... undermined Third World economic solidarity and the NIEO."[36]

Despite this, the UNCTAD Secretariat was quite energetic in its work with developing country negotiating teams within the Tokyo Round, organizing analyses and study reports as well as arranging meetings of the Group of 77. This work was fruitful to a degree in that the Tokyo Round permanently agreed on the notion of Differential and More Favorable Treatment for Developing Countries. Yet, in many respects this was the last gasp of an organization at its height. And in hindsight, this was long in coming and undermines the triumphalism of the 1970s and the NIEO years. Certainly, already by the late 1960s there was an emerging crisis in Fordism and a decline in the competitiveness of American-based productive capital (which spurred the government to devise other forms of protection for sectors facing increased foreign competition), but also the strengthening of the fractional position of money capital. Contradictions within the capitalist polity began to emerge as the consensus surrounding the post-war compromise began to unravel. While mushrooming rates of unemployment and a continual inability to resolve the crisis within the status quo framework sparked widespread labor unrest, governments in the capitalist heartland felt compelled to pursue bilateral market sharing settlements with competitors (thus undermining the multilateralist principles upon which the GATT was ostensibly predicated and upon which UNCTAD pretty much relied), and to launch what became a subsidies race in their attempt to retain a grip on their share of agricultural trade. Such a playing out from the structural crisis weakened GATT's proficiency and credibility and was to cause a major crisis for UNCTAD (see below).

At the same time, with the discarding of one of the three pillars of Bretton Woods—namely capital controls—by leading economies in the West, money capital was released from its regulation by national central banks and large amounts of (particularly American) capital were transferred to the developing world. The seeds of this went back to 1958 when the convertibility of currencies was restored in Europe with the founding of the EEC, stimulating capital mobility and imbalances in payments and destabilizing the fixed exchange rates system. By doing so, the compromise that underpinned the very structure of post-war Atlantic integration was eroded. Indeed, "the dramatic expansion in the capacity of capital to move rapidly across national and regional markets [was] intimately linked to the disruption of the Bretton Woods consensus."[37] At the same time, the retreat to unilateral behavior by Washington spurred other parties to pursue their own bilateral or regionalist agreements while increasingly retreating behind protectionist postures of varying degree. This struck at the heart of the GATT—the principle of non-discrimination—and was seen as threatening the very existence of a multilateral regime governing world trade.

This process coincided with a gradual turn in the complexity of the global economy, which further undermined both the GATT and UNCTAD's relevancy, particularly by the early 1980s. Global trade had become far more complex over the previous 40 years and the GATT and UNCTAD were unable to cope with this development. In particular the GATT's rules and regulations left it unable to adjust to the new agenda of global trade centered around trade in services—transport, travel, banking, insurance, telecommunications, consultancy and so forth. And UNCTAD's focus on commodities from the developing world could not cope with the reality that the global economy had moved on. These new forms of trade went hand-in-hand with the "third wave" of scientific innovation, i.e. the trade in ideas and knowledge intensification, ever-changing technology and innovative goods and services. These processes accelerated structural changes in the global economy and left UNCTAD's analyses and position in their wake. Certainly, meaningful North-South negotiation ended at UNCTAD V.[38]

Indeed, the organizational changes that followed the new "intellectual property" of the post-Fordist era meant that the trade in services—not included by the regulations of the GATT—was of considerable interest to more and more state elites.[39] Those particularly in the North "resented the fact that [these] newly emerging sectors such as services were left out of GATT and that the latter had little to offer in terms of intellectual property protection."[40] At the same time, the developing world bloc within UNCTAD saw the failure to include agriculture within the GATT's remit as an indication that the regime was essentially unfavorable to their developmental aspirations, particularly when loopholes in the multilateral system were heavily exploited by the North and efforts at liberalizing agricultural trade were strongly resisted by the developed world.

## Conclusion

UNCTAD's early history is one of assertion from the developing world, but then of giving ground. As the next chapter demonstrates, this became a full retreat. Such a process of Third World affirmation in the early post-colonial years and then giving ground is a replication of wider events within the global political economy and UNCTAD is not particularly unique in this. Thus as the above makes clear, a weakening of GATT persuaded its members that the very survival of a rules-based multilateral trading regime was at stake and lead to reform and reconsideration of the body. This movement towards a reformulation of the GATT occurred within the context of the rise to dominance of neoliberalism and where "monetarism and supply side economics [had] claim[ed] succession to [Keynesianism's] hegemonic aura."[41] Energy was thus channeled into addressing the issues that were seen to have undermined the GATT and constructing a revitalized and extended multilateral system. These activities led to the Uruguay Round, the Marrakech Declaration and, ultimately, the formation of the WTO. But in doing so, they caused a major crisis vis-à-vis the relevance of UNCTAD, closely tied to the fact that by the end of the 1970s it had become clear that the North was beginning to rapidly tire of UNCTAD and its demands—as well as its basic premises. Thus the historical route of UNCTAD shows a rise but then decline from some fairly assertive positions as hostility from the developed world grew. As one UNCTAD insider noted:

> The original analytical base [of UNCTAD] had been the center-periphery analysis. Northern countries despised this way of thinking. Whether right or wrong, in 1979 it became clear that in order to render negotiations successful, it would be necessary to choose a different analytical path.[42]

It is to the crises, prompted by the "new analytical path" as well as changes in the global political economy, that we now turn.

# 5 UNCTAD's crisis, retreat and reinvention

## 1980s onwards

While the heydays of the 1970s saw UNCTAD gain a great deal of international profile and prestige—something which the organization had to battle for on an almost constant basis in the face of acute hostility from the developed world—the 1980s and 1990s saw a retreat and reconfiguration of the body. This stemmed from not only Western antagonism but also from the gathering importance and influence of neoliberal ideas about how best to organize both economies and societies—something which was, it can be asserted, somewhat of the opposite to UNCTAD's established positions that emphasized the role of the state in promoting development. Consequently, UNCTAD began to reinvent itself and shift position on the big economic issues. In doing so, the organization sought to remain relevant and to escape condemnation (if not closure) by the developed world. The implications that this has had for the organization are discussed in the ensuing chapter.

### UNCTAD VI onwards

UNCTAD VI met in Belgrade in 1983 and it was from this meeting onward that one might say that the organization was on the defensive. Very little was achieved in Belgrade and the resolutions adopted were scant progress on earlier UNCTAD meetings. In fact, from UNCTAD VI we can witness a gradual acceptance by Southern elites of the overarching principles of liberalism. As with all other multilateral organizations this scenario played itself out within UNCTAD as the confrontational posturing of the 1970s gave way to more accommodatory rhetoric as the 1980s progressed—accelerating with the demise of the alternative socialist project centered in the East. This evolution is of profound importance in contextualizing UNCTAD's current positions.

The ground for this had been set back in October 1981 when 22 world leaders had met in Cancun, Mexico to discuss the issues raised in the Brandt Commission's report, *North-South*, which aimed to discuss means to overcome the deadlock in global negotiations over questions concerning trade and development. By this time, the inflexibility of the North vis-à-vis the developing world had already began to harden as neoliberalism gained momentum under Reagan and Thatcher. Cast as the "Washington Consensus," tax reform, fiscal austerity, privatization, interest rate liberalization, deregulation of products, labor, and financial markets, as well as trade liberalization, staked out what became a dominant approach to economics as the 1980s progressed.[1]

Graphically, Reagan only agreed to attend provided that Cuba was excluded; the meeting was to avoid substantive issues and was not to issue any form of final communiqué. This arrogant attitude towards the South and to broader concerns regarding development issues was compounded by Washington's behavior at the actual summit in Cancun when Reagan used the meeting as an "opportunity to lecture Third World leaders on Reaganomics and offer American technical assistance to Third World governments that wanted to emulate his domestic policies ... Afterwards, the U.S. simply refused to engage in global negotiations, forcing the North-South dialogue to a stall."[2] Such actions were applauded by Margaret Thatcher, who suggested that one of the "valuable" outcomes of Cancun was that it "was the last of such gatherings." Henceforth, "the intractable problems of Third World poverty, hunger and debt would not be solved by misdirected international intervention, but rather by liberating enterprise, promoting trade—and defeating socialism in all its forms."[3] Within this context, the future of UNCTAD looked gloomy, as the organization itself later admitted:

> A perceptible loss of confidence occurred in UNCTAD's role as a facilitator of consensus and conciliator of diverse views. Multilateral methods of dealing with international trade and development problems were eroded and several countries began to prefer a bilateral approach.[4]

Certainly, at UNCTAD VI the neoliberal government of Ronald Reagan took the offensive and came out firmly against basic propositions for a Generalized System of Preferences for developing countries. The Americans also damned UNCTAD as being "ideological." As Augelli and Murphy demonstrated, throughout the 1980s Washington (and London) actively pressurized the South into accepting the neoliberal macroeconomic policies favored by the historic bloc located in the North. This saw the focal point of power in terms of global economic governance drastically transfer to those international financial institutions where the North possessed preponderance (and hence Washington and London had fiercely rejected any notion at Cancun of putting the IMF and World Bank under United Nations (UN) control). Such a scenario had been compounded by the decision in late 1979 by the U.S. Federal Reserve Bank to raise interest rates to avoid a catastrophic decline in the dollar's value. This caused a draconian deflation in the global economy and plunged much of the South into unmanageable debt, resulting in an increased ability by the North to promote and enforce neoliberal policies onto states in grave need of financial assistance.

Those organizations struggling on behalf of the South who dared to step out of line incurred the wrath of the London-Washington axis: UNESCO, the threats against the WHO and FAO and the (enforced) inertia of the General Assembly being prime examples of an unrelenting offensive from the North against bodies that in any way seemed to challenge the prescriptions of those who controlled the global economy. Thus pressure from the United States successfully took apart the UN Center on Transnational Corporations, while also the post of director-general for International Economic Cooperation and Development was scrapped. This had been one of the most successful attempts by the South to gain a UN presence in backing international economic cooperation on development issues. However, UNCTAD was the central focus for the attack on development by the North. As Bello noted,

> [T]he focus of the northern counteroffensive was the defanging, if not dismantling, of UNCTAD. After giving in to the South during the UNCTAD IV negotiations in Nairobi in 1976 by agreeing to the creation of the commodity stabilization scheme known as the Integrated Program for Commodities, the North, during UNCTAD V in Belgrade, refused the South's program of debt forgiveness and other measures intended to revive Third World economies and thus contribute to global recovery at a time of worldwide recession.[5]

The response by UNCTAD's developing countries to this attack was restrained and in many respects emasculated. Financial indebtedness within the developing world was by this stage acting to drastically undermine sovereignty and maneuverability in the South. At the same time, leadership fractions within the South were increasingly drawn into the ongoing restructuring process as promoted by the neoliberal project, and their interests tended to be different from their own constituencies suffering from the liberalization of the developing economies. Indeed, the call for liberalization—dressed up as it was in the rhetoric of economic "realities"—gave space for conservative elements within the ruling elites of the South who had always been somewhat reluctant to commit themselves to a concrete plan of action vis-à-vis the NIEO. Their seizure upon the discourse of "economic realities" to help explain away unpopular policies reflected not only a minimal commitment to any major restructuring of the global economy (except where it benefited Southern elites), but also mirrored the tensions and contradictions inherent within an organization such as UNCTAD whose membership was so disparate. As one analyst succinctly put it:

> The ambivalence of the NIEO program . . . reflect[ed] the fact that despite rhetorical unity, the alliance that advanced this program was an uneasy one, composed of conservative, radical, and liberal states with divergent objectives. For status quo states like Mexico, world economic reform along NIEO lines was seen as a means to alleviate pressures for much-needed internal economic reforms and thus solidify the position of the ruling elites. Also, waving the NIEO flag was a perfect ideological weapon to blunt criticism from forces for change within the country.[6]

Furthermore, abandonment of "confrontational" posturing (such as the NIEO) served the interests not only of specific fractions throughout the South, but also the specific foreign policies of UNCTAD members. For example, towards the end of the 1980s the elites within Yugoslavia became aware of the pressing need to tie its economic future to the ongoing European integrationist project, particularly in light of the decline of the rest of the socialist world. Thus at the ninth summit of NAM in Belgrade in 1989, Yugoslavia "pleaded for the modernization of the Movement [thus] discarding the NAM's attitude of assertiveness vis-à-vis the two power blocs. Instead, the NAM [adopted] a more tolerant and flexible position with emphasis on cooperation and dialogue."[7] The roots of this accommodatory position were clearly reflected and revealed at UNCTAD VI. Such a position was not simply a reflection of the Yugoslavs, but reflected a playing out of the increasing integration of the world's markets and the desire by local Southern-based elites to benefit from this process wherever possible. Combative posturing against the structural inequalities of the capitalist system was seen to be of little use in facing up to globalization, particularly when—as has been pointed out—much of the elites in the South subscribed to neoliberalism. Even those that did not fully accede to this "New World Order" were painfully aware of the ongoing marginalization that much of the South was enduring and, in the words of the Indonesian ambassador to South Africa, were "willing to undertake whatever was necessary to ensure that [they] could engage the rest of the international community in dialogue."[8]

Yet the "international community" clearly set much of the agenda in the new North-South dialogue, and even while UNCTAD adopted what can be seen as a "trade unionist" approach to the world economy, discussion of the structural inequalities that underpinned the global capitalist system was quietly shelved while rhetoric concerning "economic realities," appeals to "universal standards" and claims regarding the "deideologization" of global politics became the norm. Such a process—the universalization of a particular normative agenda—within UNCTAD mirrored what was occurring in the former socialist countries and staked out the crises of the 1980s that radically reshaped UNCTAD's profile and, importantly, ideological platform. Henceforth, as the secretary-general of UNCTAD was quoted at UNCTAD VI: "What we are seeking today is not so much to negotiate new innovation in policy but rather to give effect to approaches and goals which have for long been the subject of consensus in the international community."[9] *Whose* "consensus" was left unsaid.

## The growth of neoliberalism and its effect on UNCTAD

After Belgrade, UNCTAD was forced to deal with an increasingly apparent growth in the power and reach of the private sector. At the same time, the ability to withstand the liberalizing thrust promoted by the North was further weakened by the Uruguay Round of GATT, which not only sought to lock in the developing world to the increasingly globalized world economy, but also effectively made UNCTAD's role as a discussion forum, attempting to arrive at consensus on trade issues, somewhat redundant. This was particularly so as the World Trade Organization (WTO) took on the substantive role where binding trade agreements were resolved. Ironically, it had been "global Keynesians" within UNCTAD who had "argued that the Uruguay Round . . . be capped by the transformation of GATT into a full-fledged world trade organization."[10] Equally, the Reagan administration began to aggressively take on UNCTAD. In 1984 various Western countries set up a "reflection group" to reassess their stance towards UNCTAD and how any future relationship should be crafted:

> The chief target of the US campaign was the director general of UNCTAD, Gamani Corea. A Sri Lankan national, Corea had assumed the UNCTAD helm in 1973. In a series of "green papers" about UNCTAD reform, the US campaign argued that Corea had allowed the UNCTAD staff to become top-heavy with executives committed more to North-South confrontation than to fostering trade. Furthermore, the green papers objected to the committee structure of UNCTAD, which the US felt was largely bypassed, and to UNCTAD's studies which the US felt were biased.[11]

UNCTAD then faced a crisis as Corea's tenure was coming to an end yet no agreement could be reached on his successor. To avoid a vacuum, Corea suggested that he might be willing to carry on temporarily until a successor could be found. However, Washington was resolutely opposed to such a move and was eager to get Corea out due to his political position on global development.[12] Consequently, Alister McIntyre of Grenada was named "Officer-in-Charge" of UNCTAD in December 1984 on a temporary basis. McIntyre had been deputy secretary-general of UNCTAD and "had a reputation for being a pragmatic negotiator rather than a rhetorical spokesman. His appointment was not opposed by the US."[13] Indeed, McIntyre was so close to the Americans that after the US invasion of Grenada in 1983, Washington had proposed that he be made interim leader of the island. McIntyre initially accepted, but later withdrew and stayed at UNCTAD.

Importantly, "once in office McIntyre quietly removed several of UNCTAD's more anti-Western executives from front-line positions. Although he denied that the staff changes were made in response to repeated criticism from Washington that UNCTAD's management problems were deep-seated, he eventually 'reassigned' approximately thirty senior staff."[14] As a result, pro-neoliberal reformers were placed into positions of power within UNCTAD. As the right-wing Heritage Foundation commented approvingly:

> UNCTAD has become of increasing concern to Washington policy makers who now in contrast with the 1970s, want to encourage Third World nations to try economic strategies that have a history of success [i.e., neoliberalism] . . . Recently, however, several members of the Secretariat who led the quest for a New

> International Economic Order have left UNCTAD. Gone are: Gamani Corea of Sri Lanka as UNCTAD's secretary-general; Jan Pronk, the Dutch socialist who viewed multinational corporations as neocolonial instruments of Western domination, as under-secretary-general; and Surenda Patel. Taking their places are leaders who appear to be an unexpected improvement, notable for their balance, judiciousness, and discretion.[15]

All the above raised important questions vis-à-vis the future of UNCTAD.[16] The person eventually chosen to head UNCTAD was the Ghanaian diplomat, Kenneth Dadzie. According to the Heritage Foundation, "Dadzie of Ghana served with distinction as UN Director-General for Development and International Economic Cooperation … This new leadership could transform UNCTAD from a weapon against the post-war liberal economic order into a rational organization where agreement among the developed and developing nations could be sought on the definition of trade and development problems and their solutions."[17] Dadzie certainly acted to transform UNCTAD, but in ways that suited the North and the impulses of neoliberalism. And the Heritage Foundation's ringing endorsement of Dadzie jars with other accounts. For instance, Margaret Anstee, an ex-under-secretary-general at the UN later commented on the Director-General for Development that "The people put into the job were not the most appropriate. We were thinking it should be somebody who was a Nobel Prize winner or that sort of thing—[for example] Arthur Lewis … Instead of this there was Ken Dadzie and then Jean Ribert … not exactly visionaries or strong leaders."[18]

It should be remembered that Dadzie headed the Group of 25 back in the mid-1970s—a body set up to recommend changes to the UN's economic and social sectors and to try and rectify the supposed failings of the UNDP and UNCTAD. Dadzie's recommendations included *replacing* UNCTAD with an international trade organization, provoking great unhappiness amongst the G-77 who had hoped to strengthen UNCTAD, not get rid of it. Yet this was the man who was then chosen to head UNCTAD in order to give it credibility and push through reforms. Consequently, regarded by Western officials in Geneva as pro-Western, he was "never popular with many third world delegates throughout his tenure" and "At a press conference in March 1986, he pledged that he would continue the management reforms … and took a consciously nonideological stance from the start."[19] This was all part and parcel of what had been termed the "assault on development economics."[20]

It was at UNCTAD VII in Geneva in 1987 that the new secretary-general introduced, for the very first time in UNCTAD's history, the notion that the market should play the key role in development, introducing a so-called "new spirit in North-South relations."[21] Consequently, the main concerns of UNCTAD were rethought and resources were directed at "new" issues pertaining to foreign investment and liberalization and privatization.[22] It should be pointed out that what may have concentrated the minds of UNCTAD's members was the threat by the United States "to 'kill' UNCTAD, as one observer put it, saying that the survival of UNCTAD was at the price of becoming a global OECD."[23] Such sentiments only increased as the end of the Cold War saw a radical change in the global balance of power, radically undermining what little influence the South held onto in world politics.[24]

It was in this context that the state elites (and the bureaucratic staff) within UNCTAD, sought to repackage the organization, for while the logic of neoliberalism was broadly accepted by many, the negative effects of a liberalized world were equally felt. "The new leadership [i.e., Dadzie] was chosen because it was acceptable to the US government, and those persisting in contrary views [i.e., developmentalism] left the secretariat either voluntarily or involuntarily."[25] Thus the inexorable momentum towards neoliberalism continued within the organization, provoking questions as to the continued effectiveness of UNCTAD as an instrument for the South.[26]

This process was exhibited at UNCTAD VIII in Cartagena, Colombia, in 1992 where the "Spirit of Cartagena" recognized the central roles of private enterprise and the market for growth, wrapped up in the rhetoric of "shared responsibility and partnership for development."[27] While UNCTAD's Commission remained true to its original commitment to see to the needs of the developing world, a recognition of the globalized, neoliberal normative order was implicit (and explicit) throughout the summit as:

> the texts agreed upon in Cartagena included references to a host of principles that earlier had only been championed by the OECD: an unambiguous preference for free markets; disregard of any notion of withdrawal from the world economy; an equation of democratization and the protection of human rights with development; and all the rhetoric regarding the need to decrease corruption and increase efficiency of governments in the South.[28]

For sure, this essential acceptance of the normative order was exemplified by the abandonment of any confrontational posturing in the final communiqué. Instead, the rhetoric talked of the need to "overcome confrontation and to foster a climate of genuine cooperation and solidarity" while restricting UNCTAD to the role of being basically a research body.[29] But this can be seen as part and parcel of the North's attack on UNCTAD. Bello remarked that:

> The Northern offensive escalated during UNCTAD VIII, held in Cartagena in 1992. At this watershed meeting, the North successfully opposed all linkages of UNCTAD discussions with the Uruguay Round negotiations of the General Agreement on Tariffs and Trade (GATT) and managed to erode UNCTAD's negotiation functions, thus calling its existence into question. UNCTAD's main function would henceforth be limited to "analysis, consensus building on some trade-related issues, and technical assistance."[30]

Behind the placatory rhetoric of Cartagena was an implicit recognition by the South that the globalizing impulses that shaped the contemporary world order had reduced the options, if not space, for the South to construct any viable alternative à la the NIEO.

> First, there was a change in the perception of UNCTAD, which is now to serve more to shape opinions and reach consensus rather than as a negotiating forum. Secondly, a new economic philosophy took hold which departed from old dirigistic tenets in favor of a market approach to trade and development policy and was reflected in the interpretation of UNCTAD's mission.[31]

This had profound effects on the positions of those international organizations that were ostensibly representative of the developing world, where a retreat from demands for any structural change in the global economy and a gradual and at times partial move towards the rising consensus at the elite level concerning the commonsense precepts of neoliberalism was experienced. As Hoogvelt put it post-UNCTAD VIII:

> Whereas up until that time [i.e., Cartagena] UNCTAD had been a platform where developing countries demanded adjustment of the international ... system to their developmental needs, it now expressed the belief that adoption of [neoliberal] laws and related efforts in ... GATT would facilitate technology transfers to developing countries. The structural power of transnational capital has

> not just formed the policy agenda of *deregulation*, it is also responsible for the drive to *privatization* of the state sector in all countries of the world.[32]

Acceptance of the dominant discourse while (at best) attempting to ameliorate the worst aspects of the established order hence became the tactic for much of the developing world. This was a remarkable sea change in UNCTAD's normative posture, for "until [Cartagena] UNCTAD could be viewed as a counter-hegemonic organization resisting the dominance of the Bretton Woods Institutions. The restructuring of the organization [at UNCTAD VIII gave] it a less confrontational role in the North-South dialogue."[33] Indeed, much of the South's elites had by this point begun to actively pursue neoliberal policies as a means by which their states could attempt to escape poverty. This was reflected in UNCTAD's *Trade and Development Report* of 1992 which aimed to encourage private consumption and investment demand. Yet a certain unease in some quarters over the globalization juggernaut and the neoliberal agenda was exhibited, most notably by the proposals for the application of policies with a Keynesian tinge to them to facilitate the Report's calls. Such hesitancy was reflective of the uneven adoption of neoliberalism as the path to development by some Southern elites—a scenario that was to change somewhat by the time of UNCTAD IX.

Equally of note is the fact that prior to the nomination of Rubens Ricupero, a former Brazilian finance minister, to the post in 1996, UNCTAD had been without a secretary-general for over a year. This was because there was ongoing uncertainty about the outcomes of bureaucratic reform within the UN system, as well as the UN's ongoing financial crisis. As a result, the secretary-general of the UN avoided appointing a new secretary-general of UNCTAD when the incumbent's term ended. The post was left unoccupied for 18 months, causing huge organizational disorientation and demoralization. Indeed, UNCTAD was placed in a highly invidious position, which even called into question its continued existence. Ricupero was acutely aware that UNCTAD desperately needed to prove its legitimacy and credibility, particularly to the North who were the prime funders and equally, those most skeptical of the organization's reason for existence. UNCTAD thus needed what Ricupero termed a "rebirth."[34]

Ricupero was appointed only a few months before UNCTAD IX but it was in this context, where "with the exception of Cuba and North Korea, no state … objected to the ideology of a market economy" that UNCTAD IX began, being hosted by the newly democratic

South Africa.[35] Tellingly, the theme of UNCTAD IX was "Promoting Growth and Sustainable Development in a Liberalizing and Globalizing World Economy" and it was at this conference that a definite sea change in UNCTAD's ideological orientation became clear and obvious.

## UNCTAD IX: The defining moment

The meeting in South Africa continued the broad trajectory of UNCTAD VIII. At the same time, concern was expressed from the South that the "Spirit of Cartagena" had been a largely one-sided affair, with the developing world accepting the remit of the global order, abandoning confrontational postures and calling for partnership, while the developed world did very little to reciprocate. Yet, in an era of the WTO the ability of UNCTAD to promote changes in the global economic environment was rigorously critiqued by the developed world, particularly as many Northern-based elites strongly wished to avoid taking clear positions on matters that the WTO handled. Indeed, questions regarding how UNCTAD related to the WTO emerged as paramount concerns of the North at the summit, as the developed world sought to further limit the role UNCTAD had to play in any economic ordering of the global economic architecture.

Thus as UNCTAD IX progressed, it became clear that the North opposed any reference to the implementation of "specific WTO agreements, especially if developing countries suggested that their developed counterparts were not honoring their obligations," while vigorously maneuvering against "granting UNCTAD a specific mandate in [various] areas, particularly the notion that UNCTAD should take up and examine issues before they are taken up in the WTO."[36] The North also opposed references to intellectual property rights already agreed upon by the WTO, apparently fearing that the South was trying to renegotiate already concluded articles, even if such agreements were not in their interests. Importantly, many "developed countries were reluctant both to allow UNCTAD to examine their macroeconomic policies and its impact on the global economy, and to continue its work on behalf of developing countries with regard to debt management."

Emboldened by the dominant status of neoliberalism as *the* normative economic model and the perennial weakness of a South which had abandoned demands for a NIEO in favor of "partnership," the capitalist North was essentially in no mood for compromise, rejecting any terms that hinted at new financial responsibilities, such as propositions to erect financing devices and trust funds for the South. Even condemnation of unilateralism and extraterritorial measures were stalled, as Washington saw this as an attack on their policies towards Havana and Baghdad. Essentially the North—as a British government briefing paper put it—wanted at the very least UNCTAD "reformed" and relegated to undertaking "policy analysis and research into trade and developmental issues," and to abstain from "very general concerns such as interdependence, in favor of specific, targeted types of work in key areas."[37] At the same time, heads of disciplinary institutions such as the WTO (its director-general), the IMF (its managing director), and the World Bank (its managing director) played a prominent role in the proceedings—a manifestation of a move away from social concerns to much narrower conceptions of what constitutes global economic competitiveness.

Reflecting the changed times and new agenda of what had formerly been the developing world's voice against such Northern-dominated organizations, UNCTAD's secretary-general thanked the WTO's head for attending and asserted that his presence had been a concrete expression of the evolving cooperation between the two organizations. This cooperative attitude—arguably pursued to keep the organization "relevant"—between UNCTAD and its former ostensible protagonists was reflected in the final Midrand Declaration.

The Midrand Declaration was formulated and drafted by the conference's president, South Africa's minister of trade and industry, Alec Erwin, in consultation with delegations at UNCTAD IX.[38] A number of notable elements of the Declaration are worthy of discussion. First, the document was grounded very much within the ongoing discourse and world order. The WTO was referred to as having "strengthened the rules-based trading system and furthered the process of liberalization," while such a scenario was claimed as "opening new opportunities for sustainable development and growth." The Declaration also asserted that UNCTAD IX had "responded to these changes and challenges" by attempting to "give new and real meaning to the partnership for development." Market forces were said to "play a pivotal role," while the WTO was claimed to "facilitate [the] positive integration of countries into the global trading system."[39]

With acceptance of the norms of trade liberalization went a recognition of the uneven and unequal process of globalization. This translated into a call for an attempt at lessening the worst aspects of this process. Thus the principles of the "Spirit of Cartagena" were reinforced with a renewed call for "partnership for development." Reflecting the South's unease at the North's somewhat tardy response to their willingness to construct a modus vivendi, the Midrand Declaration pointedly remarked that such partnership had to be grounded on a clear definition of roles, common objectives and *joint* action.

This was envisaged as involving the intensification of intergovernmental cooperation between North and South; South-South cooperation; a more effective coordination and complementarity of multilateral institutions; an increased dialogue between governments and civil society aimed at facilitating development; and a renewed "partnership" between public and private sectors in order to achieve increased economic growth rates and ergo (according to the Declaration) greater development. Following on from this, South Africa (as president of UNCTAD) agreed to host a workshop on this expected partnership between public and private sectors, in particular on how to encourage the private sector in more advanced developing countries to assist those least developing nations. This was changed, at the behest of the UNCTAD Secretariat, to refocus the workshop to concentrate on the "definition, development and consolidation of a *positive* agenda for LDCs (and low income countries in preparation for WTO negotiations" [emphasis added].[40] Held in late June 1999, the meeting sought to enhance the least developing countries' participation in making global trade rules at the WTO.

Returning to UNCTAD IX, Pretoria's delegation ostensibly negotiated on a common platform agreed upon with the Africa Group and, more broadly, as part of the G77. Yet, as South Africa's deputy director of foreign trade relations later asserted, "it sought to build bridges among all member countries in an attempt to achieve overall consensus."[41] This role was later celebrated by a senior DFA official who saw South Africa as "in the middle" and having "breathed new life into UNCTAD at UNCTAD IX" by indicating that it was "seriously interested in a meaningful debate and engagement with the North."[42] Its "bridgebuilding" role then helped convince many Southern elites at the conference of the desirability to avoid confrontational rhetoric and agree to the notion of "partnership" with the North. In some regards, this sought to change the culture of UNCTAD away from "begging" and towards taking more responsibility for economic malperformance.[43] For sure, many delegations already shared an acceptance of the tenets of neoliberalism, but Pretoria's tactical activities were of profound importance at the meeting and at the closing plenary, much mention was made of the constructive way in which the South African team transposed the country's experience and "spirit" of negotiated compromise during sessions dealing with controversial aspects of the pre-conference text.

This consensus building by Pretoria accounted for much of the rhetoric of "success" which greeted the closing of UNCTAD IX with the claim that "every member state felt that its views were reflected in the Conference's final text and the Midrand Declaration" and that "a win-win outcome" had resulted.[44] Much of this was cast as UNCTAD gaining new-found "credibility" with the developed world.[45] Yet the celebratory rhetoric contradicted an earlier position of UNCTAD's secretary-general, who had cautioned an overly enthusiastic embrace of neoliberalism.

At the same time, a deeper malaise for the South was evident at the conference as state elites scrambled to attract investment from the North. Certainly UNCTAD IX was marked by a great deal of bilateral negotiations behind closed doors between individual countries of the South and the developed world. In what may be viewed as a rush for the best deal in a situation where Southern solidarity against the negative effects of globalization and transnational capital was manifestly absent, individual state elites attempted to fashion agreements on an individual basis. Indeed South Africa was reported to have arranged a large number of trade pacts with various European and Asian states at the conference. In a situation where, as the special adviser to South Africa's minister of trade and industry argued, UNCTAD IX was sending "out a message that developing countries are going to take full responsibility for their development," the reasoning of competing for investment with little regard for an overarching normative framework on how to best coordinate this process seemed logical, if not overly desirable.

## Criticism of UNCTAD IX

This position, though celebrated in some quarters as marking a "consensus" and a new "reality" in North-South relations along with a concomitant congratulation to Pretoria on its "positive" contribution to UNCTAD IX as a "bridgebuilder," was, however, critiqued in other quarters. Indeed Hormeku suggested that post-Midrand it was evident that:

> UNCTAD was losing its direction and spirit as guardian and defender of the development principle and perspective, and was trying to "mature" into an agency seeking "consensus." Since the prevailing consensus is the free-market liberalization model that is promoted by the Bretton Woods Institutions and the WTO, UNCTAD seems to be seeking a role to be relevant to this model

> and to be accepted, for instance, by the WTO and the International Chamber of Commerce, rather than to challenge or provide alternatives to the model.[46]

The Midrand Declaration's emphasis on partnership with the private sector as a tool for development was also criticized as promoting the idea that foreign investment was "the panacea to solve every problem." Furthermore, the "consensus" so carefully crafted at UNCTAD IX was cast as "the ideology of pragmatism" yet "in the present international context, this meant supporting the intense international competition for markets in which states have little control over their own economies."[47] Such a "consensus" on economic policy served to fetishize the market and elevate growth as an end in itself.

Certainly after UNCTAD IX, development ran the risk of being measured by macroeconomic indicators and levels of investment, rather than the overall condition of society. Such a scenario suited the interests of the North, now that good governance and commonsense attitudes to market-friendly policies, rather than dealing with the broader underpinnings of the international political economy, were regarded as the key to development. In short, UNCTAD IX under South Africa's chairmanship, continued and extended the move away from questioning the overall global situation and how this structurally affects development, and towards the more "pragmatic" position of making economies in the South as attractive as possible to foreign investors. As one senior official remarked, "South Africa encourages developing countries to get their act together" regarding global trade. By doing so, Pretoria attempted to "lead by example" in restructuring its economy along neoliberal lines.[48] Still, it is hard to disagree with the assertion that "the reason for [UNCTAD's] establishment and existence was to champion and advocate the perspective of development and of the South, and not be a consensus-seeking agency with a niche of being 'relevant' to the agenda of donor agencies or to be an appendant to the WTO."[49] This latter issue will be discussed later. But at this point it can be stated that while the "Spirit of Cartagena" proclaimed a makeover of North-South relations towards a more uniform global trading system, UNCTAD IX and the Midrand Declaration brought about a completely novel approach to North-South dialogue in the form of "partnership for development," which strongly advocated partnerships with the private sector. UNCTAD IX resulted in the organization abandoning its historic opposition to the global capitalist system and rather reinvented the body within the structures and context of neoliberal globalization.

Having said that, it is debatable whether UNCTAD had any choice. By the mid-1990s the organization was facing a huge credibility gap as well as serious questions vis-à-vis its relevance. These had in particular been highlighted by the *Report on Global Governance* in 1990 and Maurice Bertrand's 1995 suggestions for UN reform, which had introduced the idea of an Economic Security Council. Both reports would have made UNCTAD completely irrelevant. And there were plenty of opinions within Northern governments that UNCTAD should indeed die a death. So from this context, reinventing UNCTAD was crucial and, as a result of Midrand, UNCTAD was transformed from being a radical critique of global capitalism and its framers, to being an apparatus of global economic governance. Certainly, UNCTAD could be said to have abandoned its traditional role of providing a serious counterbalance to the economic prescriptions of the North.[50]

## UNCTAD X

UNCTAD X was held in Bangkok, Thailand in 2000 under the rubric of "Development Strategy in the Interdependent World." Of note, Thailand was one of the countries which had been most affected by the Asian Crisis of 1997. Equally important, UNCTAD X was the first major conference on global economic issues after the debacle of the third WTO ministerial meeting in Seattle, which had supposedly launched the "Millennium Round." Consequently, UNCTAD X focused on WTO-related issues.

The conference was characterized by a limited recognition, absent in large measure from recent UNCTAD meetings, that development objectives had to be placed at the core of the globalization process. Indeed, one of the features of UNCTAD X was an expressed concern regarding the glaring imbalances incumbent with globalization. It must be remembered that UNCTAD X came very soon after the collapse of the WTO meeting in Seattle in November 1999 and it was within this context that some space seemed to open up for a more resolute stance vis-à-vis the pace and thrust of globalization. However, this should not be exaggerated as perhaps one of the main reasons why discussion regarding neoliberal globalization in Bangkok was so ostensibly "free" was because UNCTAD had been progressively stripped of any teeth. Indeed, UNCTAD's secretary-general, Rubens Ricupero, admitted as much, saying that debate could be more expressive as "the organization ... does not set rules on trade or investment, has no enforcement authority and does not resolve disputes involving the national interests of its members."[51] In other words, very little is at stake and the North's interests are not in any way under threat. This was amply evidenced by the fact that neither the European Union nor the US even bothered sending senior trade officials to the meeting. In addition, it is true that after Seattle there was a greater receptiveness to the developing world's concerns and a recognition that a nascent backlash against globalization was in the offing. But, antipathies evidenced by elite delegations from the developing world at UNCTAD X reflected a variety of positions of often-contradictory agendas. These ranged from the demand for sweeping global reform, to special treatment for Southern exporters, to equal treatment for the same. However, as had been evident for a good time now, what most developing world delegations demanded at such multilateral meeting points was increased access to the world market for externally oriented fractions. Far from "stopping" neoliberal globalization, the elites from the developing world push for greater integration into the global capitalist order.

Consequently, many of the positions advanced in Bangkok amounted to little more than strategies to defend neoliberal globalization from the sort of populist counter-hegemonic impulses evidenced in Seattle. This is not to say that representatives from the developing world do not express genuine grievances at forums such as UNCTAD. But, such expressions remain hidebound by an essential acceptance of the logic of a global "free market" which just needs tampering with here and there to make globalization "work" for development. It is this confused position from the developing world, combined with an obstinate refusal by the North to seriously negotiate substantive issues within the ambit of UNCTAD, that meant that the Declaration emanating from the Bangkok meeting was considerably ambiguous and lacking in any clear statement. In fact, the 52-page Plan of Action adopted at the end of the Bangkok meeting had nothing to say on how future talks at the WTO should be framed but was little more than a synopsis of ongoing debates on global trade, finance, and investment.

Indeed, UNCTAD X put forward only general expressions of hope that North and South *might* in due time arrange some sort of agreement to promote both globalization and development. Thus the Bangkok Declarations talked of how it was "essential to persevere in the search for consensual solutions," without going into any meaningful detail as to what these were.[52] In particular, the Bangkok meeting failed to resolve the demand by developing nations that the developed world open up their markets fully to their products, without tariff barriers. The North's position was to pledge a "possible commitment" to free access for "essentially all" exports from the Least Developed Countries.[53] European delegates in particular were keen to claim that "essentially all" meant 99 percent of the LDC's products. However, cynics—probably correctly—noted that the missing 1 percent would unquestionably include "difficult" exports that might impact upon important sectors such as textiles and agriculture, which are, as is well known, provided with intense protectionism (contra neoliberal dogma) due to powerful domestic constituencies. Devoid of meaningful content, both the Declaration and Plan of Action from UNCTAD X was little more than a collection of seemingly innocuous statements on the importance of development and poverty reduction, laced with vague assertions that free market globalization "should" provide benefits to all.

## UNCTAD XI

The eleventh ministerial meeting of the United Nations Conference on Trade and Development was held from 13–18 June 2004 in Sao Paulo, Brazil. The main theme of UNCTAD XI was "Enhancing the coherence between national development strategies and global economic processes towards economic growth and development, particularly of developing countries." Remarkably, given the past conferences and the general disappointments for many activists, UNCTAD XI ended in what Martin Khor of Third World Network characterized as "a rather good spirit."[54] The conference adopted the "Sao Paulo Consensus," which included detailed analyses of globalization, trade and development issues, as well as policy proposals. The future role of UNCTAD was also enunciated.

The Sao Paulo Consensus was concerned primarily with development strategies in the context of a globalizing world; developing productive capacities; fostering development gains from the global trading system; and "partnerships for development." The most important feature of the Consensus was the expressed need for what was termed "policy space." Countries of the South argued that they needed this space to devise their own developmental strategies and a degree of flexibility to advance their own policies. The rules associated with the WTO and the dominance of neoliberal thought and practice were deemed to be constraining this space. The North in turn was alarmed that any acknowledgment of the right of Southern countries to "policy space" would fortify the South's bargaining position vis-à-vis the North and possibly enable them to resist further pressure for continued liberalization and privatization, particularly within the WTO but also in resisting IFI structures centered around conditionalities.

The issue was decided in paragraph 8 of the Consensus which recognized that "it is particularly important for developing countries, bearing in mind their development goals and objectives, that all countries take into account the need for appropriate balance between national policy space and international disciplines and commitments." The text also stated that:

> the increasing interdependence in a globalizing world and the emergence of rule-based international economic regimes have meant that the space for national economic policy (especially in trade, investment and industrial development) is now often framed by international disciplines, commitments and global market considerations. It is for each government to evaluate the trade-off between the benefits of accepting international rules and commitments and the constraints posed by the loss of policy space.

This paragraph on "policy space" was the first time that the notion that developing countries needed policy space (particularly in the milieu of intrusive global rules) had been accepted. Thus Paragraph 21 originally stated, "at the national level, the important elements for growth and development include political stability, transparent and accountable governance, and the rule of law." Instead, the South succeeded in getting Paragraph 21 to read, "good governance within each country *and at the international level* is essential for sustained growth and development" [emphasis added].

Equally important for the South was Paragraph 10, which stated that as the chosen site for trade and development issues, UNCTAD has a particular duty to play a role in achieving the Millennium Development Goals (MDGs). This was a de facto rejection of the Northern position that wanted UNCTAD relegated to having a technocratic advisory role at the *national* level, as opposed to its current and ongoing role of policy research and analysis on global trading issues. The Consensus thus rebutted the desire by the North to weaken UNCTAD's independent role in regard to the Bretton Woods institutions in its research and analysis.

Of note were the messages from people such as Brazilian President Luiz Lula da Silva, Thai Premier Thaksin, and UN secretary-general Kofi Annan who all urged developing countries to rely more on themselves through South-South trade. This was perhaps the most notable feature to come out of UNCTAD XI. And indeed the impetus from leaders of the South for South-South trade and cooperation to build solidarity was specifically aimed at lessening dependence on the North. This reflected the fact that bargaining coalitions, particularly at the WTO but also at other multilateral sites, are of increasing interest and importance in advancing negotiating positions in the emerging global trade regime.[55] The G-20 position sprang from a realization that subsidies in the developed world will not simply disappear through goodwill but require strong lobbying, political pressure and organization from those interested countries. Implicit in the creation of the G-20 is an understanding that negotiations have not worked so far and have perhaps served to prolong the existing situation. In other words, the G-20 has emerged due to a fundamental distrust held by the developing, agriculturally inclined nations, vis-à-vis the industrialized stance towards free trade in agricultural products.[56] The G-20 is thus using neoliberal positions within the WTO to delegitimize the position of the North.

In essence, the G-20 were incensed by the moves made by the US and EU prior to Cancun which, rather than maintaining the Doha Declaration, wanted to safeguard subsidy regimes in return for negligible reforms and also pushed for the "Singapore issues" to be discussed. These were those issues that the industrialized countries wished to negotiate, namely global rules governing investment, competition policies, transparency in government procurement processes and the coordination of customs procedures. Prior to Cancun, Brazil, Argentina and India thus set up an alliance to push for negotiations in line with the commitments made at Doha, with South Africa, Nigeria, Egypt, China, Mexico and most of Latin America also joining up. It can be inferred from such a move that work within the structures of the WTO had not resolved matters to the satisfaction of key elites in the developing world. What this also meant was that this grouping accounted for over 20 percent of the globe's agricultural GDP, 26 percent of total agricultural exports, 51 percent of the world's population and 63 percent of all farmers—a not insignificant grouping in other words. This formation can be perhaps seen as a watershed in global trade politics as developing countries were taking the lead in promoting free and fair trade within a liberalized framework. As Brazil's President, Luiz Inácio Lula da Silva, remarked, "At Cancún, no one believed the G21 (developing nations) [i.e., G-20] could create such an impact. But we did, which makes us believe 20 countries representing more than half the world's population, can change rules of the world trade."[57] The implications for UNCTAD of this grouping, which stands apart from the organization, are interesting. Does this now mean that developing world ambitions are to be advanced via informal groupings within the WTO but outside UNCTAD structures? This so far looks the case.

Central to the G-20's existence is the importance of a predictable, rule-based, and transparent multilateral trading system as a means through which developing countries can maximize their development via trade and their competitive advantage. As Corea has asserted, the WTO

> is an irreplaceable organization. We need it. We need it badly. We need a strong WTO and from the perspective of developing countries, this is really an irreplaceable forum—with all its shortcomings, with all its problems—this is where [the G-20] can make a difference. We can get some predictability. We can get some rules and we can get some enforceable rules in an area where in the past we had none.[58]

Thus, as Kirsty Nowlan, World Vision's delegate at Cancun noted, "The emergence of the G-20 as a strong force on the negotiating scene represents a sea change in the way developing countries approach the WTO. It is the first time they have used their potential power as a negotiating block to balance out negotiations."[59] Interestingly, UNCTAD is wholly absent from such discussions.

Aside from this broader context, other states are increasingly developing ties with the less-developed world, creating axes that bypass and perhaps in the long run may threaten American dominance, but also bypass UNCTAD. China is clearly more and more keen to establish special relationships with regional powers in the developing world and in particular, in Africa.[60] This in particular has the potential that such overlapping developments may come together and create a nascent bloc of the developing world to forge greater participation in the global trading system—particularly its regulation—as well as providing alternatives to simple North-South directions in trade. Indeed, the G-20 might be seen as nascent attempts to create a "new trade geography" which does not ignore the primary importance of trade with the G-8 but does at the same time seek to restructure global trade along liberal lines. The growth of trade ties among developing countries has the possibility of democratizing global trade relations and may help rein in the current domination of the United States—something which clearly worries Washington, as its aggressive reaction to the G-20 demonstrates. The India-Brazil-South Africa (IBSA) Dialogue Forum is another potential grouping of note.[61] Yet it has to be remembered that all this takes place—in stark contrast to the 1970s—with very little input from UNCTAD.

Importantly, the initiatives are not simply spoilers in the WTO process. "These initiatives are not to be seen as a revival of the third-world movement of the 1960s and 1970s. None of their declarations openly question the principles of liberal economic globalization. But the agreements do start a new phase in a process that has continued since 1945: the South's gradual self-assertion on the world stage."[62]

However, it should be flagged that it is a measure of the basic liberal underpinnings of the G-20's diplomacy that conservative newspapers such as South Africa's *Business Day* can endorse Pretoria's (and by implication the G-20's) policies with some enthusiasm (while at the same time making it clear that this is not a return to the days of the NIEO):

> In talking, as he did repeatedly on his US tour, of the need for a "massive transfer of resources" to Africa, Mbeki may, to some ears, have sounded like a chairman of the Non-Aligned Movement from the 60s demanding reparations for the evils of colonialism. But that was emphatically not what he was saying. He was talking about transfers *based on market principles.* To be sure, old-fashioned, but better channeled, assistance was still needed. But the really important thing was that Africa be unshackled to attract greatly expanded investment and technology flows, generate jobs and revenue from trade, and reap the benefits of globalization.[63]

Yet while the reformist positions of the G-20 might well be the policies of pragmatism in the present international context, this means in the final analysis advocating the intensification of international competition for markets in which states have relatively limited control over their own economies. Related to this is the conundrum facing the G-20, namely what strategy exists within the commonsense approach adopted by the group vis-à-vis global trade to both promote greater exports and market access for agri-business *and* protect the peasantry and small farmers of many of the G-20's members? UNCTAD's years of research on such matters seem to be ignored. Thus apparent from G-20 statements is the absence of positions on protecting markets or steadying primary commodity prices. So, whether or not the group can both liberalize and safeguard domestic interests outside of the agro-exporting fractions remains an unanswered and indeed, unexplored, question—something which UNCTAD could have probably helped on.

Keeping together a broad-based coalition, such as the G-20, may prove to be very difficult. Moving forward necessitates that the G-20 chooses which subjects at the WTO they should negotiate on and also implies, given resource constraints and the lack of capacity (again, something which UNCTAD could help), that key states from the developing world take a lead. But this is much easier said than done and serves to flag caution. Consolidating incompatible interests within any such developing world grouping such as the G-20 is highly problematic and while Pretoria or Brasilia may argue (or even think) that what is good for South Africa or Brazil is good for the rest of their respective continents, others may not think so and may even be highly suspicious of intentions.

It is true that "What we are looking at is a shift in paradigm, an inverting of roles with developing nations now heading the fight for trade liberalization in the face of resistance from rich countries."[64] But, any critical positioning of the G-20 is offset by a broader acceptance of the orthodoxy of neoliberalism and the G-20's limited scope, which is largely focused on agricultural trade liberalization, and the implicit reluctance to expand the group's concerns regarding globalization's effects beyond the push for further trade liberalization, restricts the transformative potentiality of developments so far. The decades of UNCTAD research and policy positions have been thrown out of the window in this regard. While there are clear limitations to the G-20 developing into a nascent opportunity through which an alternative power bloc might be developed, strategic space that has opened up in the last five years or so will remain under-utilized as long as the initiatives remain so constricted in scope.

It can be argued that the emergence of the G-20 demonstrates that the retreat of the developing world, which staked out the 1980s and 1990s, and which saw "America's quest for hegemony" may be in abeyance as globalization is being seen to be more and more one-sided.[65] But this pregnant agenda needs broadening beyond its current narrow confines. It does of course have to be noted that only a small number of the WTO's members actually have the capacity and indeed bargaining power to push forward complex trade negotiations, particularly on the key issue of market access (the majority of African countries, for instance, are actually quite woeful on this score). Cancun seemed to show that an effective counter-balance to the G-8 could be found in a group of the large and dynamic developing countries coming together. From this phenomenon, it may be argued that an emerging bloc of powers within the global trading regime may be nascent. However, we should be aware that "unlike the third-world movements of the 1960s and 1970s, the G-20 does not explicitly challenge the international economic system, nor propose an alternative social model. It is still too early to envisage any fundamental changes to the power relationships that structure international society."[66] And the actions of Brazil and India at Hong Kong militate against any over-enthusiasm for the G-20 as it is currently constructed. After all, "It is paradoxical that the G-20, whose formation captured the imagination of the developing world during the Cancun ministerial, has ended up being the launching pad for India and Brazil's integration into the WTO power structure."[67]

## Conclusion

Whether the G-20 and the blossoming call for a reformed global trading order can move forward and beyond the current global impasse, and in effect try to tip the global scales back into balance (something which UNCTAD tried and failed at in the 1970s), will be of extreme interest in the future. While we may not be witnessing a rebirth of the NIEO, interesting times seem to await us with regard to the management of the international system. It is true that at Cancun, the talks ended before any substantial negotiations on the draft agriculture text, so the strength of G-20 cohesion was not tested, however, interactions involving the G-20 in the WTO will probably continue to be sites of an important ongoing debate and, it could be argued, the testing—if not reformulating—of important global balances. As one commentator noted, "As long as the WTO exists as a Western-driven unreformed regulator of global discipline it will face resistance for its institutional and moral failures. The message from Cancún is clear: a strong Southern framework can give poorer nations more time and space to defend themselves and the hope of negotiating a more equitable deal for their peoples."[68] The emerging coalitions of developing countries within the ambit of the WTO are developments that will be of profound interest in future trade rounds—but where UNCTAD fits into this is of great doubt.

Indeed, these developments have taken place with little reference to UNCTAD and it seems apparent that developing nations, particularly the leading ones, are staking out policies and positions without consulting UNCTAD nor using UNCTAD as a particularly important site from which their visions can be enunciated. In short, the action with regard to development has moved to the WTO and in particular to alliance-building activities and coalitions that although nominally linked to the G-77 and thus to UNCTAD in reality have little connection. The relevance of UNCTAD within this milieu is thus in question, something that is turned to in the next chapter.

# 6 The multilateral trading system and the future

## Where does UNCTAD fit into the WTO?

One of the key challenges that UNCTAD has faced in recent years has been its continuing raison d'etre in a world trading regime dominated and supervised by the World Trade Organization (WTO). Indeed, the existence of the WTO has in the past been used to argue for the disbandment of UNCTAD—and the North periodically raises this specter if and when UNCTAD challenges its favored positions on global trading negotiations and arrangements.

This chapter seeks to examine those matters that have influenced the workings of UNCTAD, contextualized within a WTO-driven trading regime. The relationship that UNCTAD has with the WTO is of crucial importance vis-à-vis the future role(s) of UNCTAD and how it fits within the overarching global governance architecture. From the days of UNCTAD I the organization has had to contend with problems associated with its doubts over its very existence and has had to perpetually make a great effort in attaining credit and credibility as an institutional body in negotiating trade conventions and basic principles. The problems that UNCTAD has faced stem from the fact that the GATT was previously in existence before UNCTAD was formed and had been the body that set the task of presenting negotiating frameworks in trading relations with the backing of the developed countries, i.e. the major trading powers.

### Background to UNCTAD and the WTO

As discussed in Chapters 3 and 4, there have been continued divergences and issues between the GATT and the IFIs and UNCTAD. This has centered around the place that developing countries' priorities have within the GATT system (as well as within the IFIs) and more broadly, the ideologies of development that drive policies and how such policies should influence global trade relations and concomitantly, development in the South. As seen in Chapters 3 and 4, neoliberal ideas have increasingly underpinned the IFIs—and latterly UNCTAD itself—and despite UNCTAD's rearguard actions in this regard, liberal ideas vis-à-vis growth and development (in that order) now generally dominate discussions within the organization. The days when UNCTAD challenged the North's norms around the global trading architecture are over, certainly compared to the heydays of the NIEO.

The historical (and current) problem facing UNCTAD—and particularly its developing country members—is that all chief resolutions and decisions passed by UNCTAD are dependent upon the agreement of the IFIs for implementation. As a result, the most that UNCTAD can do is press for the modification of such rules and frameworks, utilizing the widespread legitimacy that UNCTAD possesses in the eyes of the developing world. In this sense, UNCTAD plays an, at best, moderating influence on the IFIs, although the core and substantive issues around global trade are pretty much beyond the reach of the organization, at least in practical terms. Consequently, UNCTAD has more and more taken on the role of pressing for the amelioration of the more negative aspects of globalization and for pushing the developed world to come good on their liberalizing messages. In short, UNCTAD's relationship with organizations such as the WTO is one of promoting equitable implementation and seeking to raise the concerns of the South. But this has more and more been acted upon within the basic premises of neoliberal globalism, rather than confronting or challenging such norms as was arguably the case during the NIEO days. UNCTAD can perhaps therefore be characterized as a reformist international pressure group rather than an international organization with clout.

UNCTAD's influence on the IFIs is highly constrained and its arguments, although often based on ethical positions (which in itself is not a dishonorable situation) are frequently ignored. Indeed, UNCTAD's positions may generally only be granted by the developed countries if the cost is not too high for the North. Beyond that, UNCTAD's ability to influence global trading relations is highly limited. This is not the least because the type of policy research and technical activities that takes up the bulk of UNCTAD's work is, in the main, dependent on funding from the North. Actions and policies that might say the opposite to neoliberal norms backed by the North are thus unwelcome and unlikely—indeed are positively discouraged, even if only implicitly. UNCTAD's exact relationship with the WTO is something which we now turn to in fuller detail.

## UNCTAD and its engagement with the WTO

The creation of the WTO was the most serious attempt yet to restructure the international political economy and established what may be viewed as the premier disciplinary agent of global capitalism as it is currently organized, viz. neoliberalism. Its founding has had serious implications for all actors in the international political economy. The flexibility and practicality that had marked much of the GATT's regime, which was cognizant of the difficulties faced by administrations in liberalizing their markets, has been removed. Strict institutionalization of normative principles regarding the functioning of the global economy is now enshrined. Such institutionalization has had profound implications for UNCTAD as an organization, grappling as it does with the South's place in the global political economy.

In November 1982 in Geneva, a ministerial meeting of GATT members attempted to launch an important new round of negotiations. Though the conference ultimately failed—brought down by disputes surrounding the agriculture issue—the work program that the Geneva meeting had agreed to, came to provide the basis of the negotiating agenda for what was to become known as the "Uruguay Round." Despite this, it took another four years before the various administrations agreed to launch the new round of negotiations, doing so in September 1986, in Punta del Este in Uruguay. The gathered ministers eventually accepted a negotiating agenda that subsequently covered virtually every outstanding trade policy issue. The talks were going to extend the trading system into several new areas, notably trade in services and intellectual property, and to reform trade in the sensitive sectors of agriculture and textiles. All the original GATT articles were up for review.

Space precludes an examination of the intricate negotiations that led to the formation of the WTO.[1] What shall be briefly commented upon are the fundamental principles that the Marrakech Declaration outlined, and in particular how these affect the South and indirectly, UNCTAD's positions.

On 15 April 1994 the Marrakech Declaration was signed, paving the way for the formation of the WTO. From the beginning the Declaration was a compromise that protected the North's agricultural sector. Lobbyists for the European agricultural industry had strongly resisted any deal which posed a threat to their protected position, while agricultural producers outside of Europe were very reluctant to sign a deal which did not tackle the reform of the European market and a halt to its noncompetitive behavior. In short, the Declaration was a compromise and in "instances where the choice was between risking serious conflict and attempting to enforce the letter of GATT disciplines—for example on regional integration or subsidies—the contracting parties generally 'blinked.'"[2] This being said, the WTO put forward a radical and far-reaching agenda for the future regulation of world trade.

### *Services*

Previously GATT had primarily focused on the trade in goods. As has been commented upon, this was rapidly superseded in the 1980s by a massive growth in the proportion of world output and trade being situated in services, such as finance, telecommunications, tourism and the media. The Uruguay Round sought to apply the same principles to services trade as applied to goods (such as most favored nation and nondiscrimination). At the heart of the General Agreement on Trade in Services (GATS) was the effective commodification of financial services and the extension of legal obligations to free capital movement, which essentially overrode national economic sovereignty. At the same time, "the definition of exports [was] extended in the case of services to include production by foreign owned subsidiaries in the host country. Trade regulation [was] thus ... extended for the first time to the internal market regimes of member states."[3]

### *Agriculture*

Terms of the agreement encompassed market access, internal supports and subsidized exports. New regulations on sanitary standards were to be introduced in the North over a six-year period while food-importing states were granted 10 years. Least developed countries were exempt. This deal, known as the Agreement on Sanitary and Phytosanitary Measures was designed to reduce the ability of states—often heavily influenced by a disproportionately powerful agricultural lobby—to use sanitary standards as a barrier to imports.

As an industry notorious for its amount of nontariff barriers, these were to undergo a process of "tariffication," i.e. to be converted to tariffs. Developed countries were committed to reducing tariffs by 36 percent over six years, while developing countries must reduce them by 24 percent over 10 years (primary staples being exempted). Exceptions remained, but the deal was the first concerted success in liberalizing trade in agricultural products.

Yet the effect of these measures will be uneven throughout the South. The reduction of export subsidies by Europe and the United

States will make those countries that also export similar agricultural products more competitive as their costs are cheaper—their market share is expected to rise. A study by the OECD-World Bank has estimated that prices for many foodstuffs (wheat, maize, barley, meat and dairy products etc.) will rise by up to 7 percent. While food-exporting countries will benefit from this development, net importers—very often the least developed states—will suffer, as UNCTAD has repeatedly noted. Certainly, any rise in the cost of food imports will compound the difficulties of the debt-burdened states—those that can least afford such an outcome.

### *Textiles*

Under the Multi-Fiber Arrangement of 1961, limitations on the amount of textiles imported into developed countries from the South had acted as effective taxes on the developing world's exports. Under the rubric of the WTO, these quotas will be phased out over a period of 10 years. This will have a mixed effect on the developing world, for while relatively efficient textile producers will be freed from the effective taxes imposed on them by the MFA when exporting to the North (industries in states such as China, Thailand, India and South Africa stand to gain), less efficient textile producers—largely concentrated in Central America and the Caribbean—will lose out unless their productivity is raised.[4] Of course, how this "competitiveness" is achieved is highly controversial, though usually one of the first casualties is labor as "flexibility" and a lowering of "costs" is high on the agenda. This invariably results in increased job insecurity, the repression of labor rights and the intensification of the exploitation of females.[5]

Furthermore the phasing out of the quotas on imports from the developing world is slow (10 years) and in that period the scramble in the South to position themselves as the most "competitive" in order to place their exports in the markets of the North is likely to become a "race to the bottom" for the average textile worker in developing countries. This is particularly so in an era where the ability to compete at all costs undermines any residual sympathy the elites in the South may have had for its working class. After all, often the only competitive advantage poorer states possess is their destitution and the ability to produce with minimal labor costs, while the elites see investment as the solution to all their problems, as well as a possible source of enrichment via "deals." Any labor unrest that threatens this is likely to provoke repression—textile-producing Bangladesh is a classic example of all of these points.

### *Tariffs*

Once the Uruguay Round is fully implemented, tariffs on imports of industrial products by the developed world will fall from an average of 6.4 percent to just 4.0 percent. Nontariff barriers—quotas and subsidies—will be converted to tariffs and then progressively eliminated through scheduled reductions.

### *Trade Related Intellectual Property Rights (TRIPs)*

Though intellectual property rights had been covered by the 132-member World Intellectual Property Organization since 1967, the TRIPs proviso went much further and covered patents, copyright and trademarks. Supporters of the provisions were all states located in the developed world and based their argument on the grounds that protection stimulated research and development, i.e. there is little incentive to engage in research if the new inventions that spring from this process cannot be protected from rival competitors. Hence states that established an effective protection for intellectual property rights were more likely to be recipients of investment from companies anxious about the illicit duplication of their intellectual property.

Opposition to this position was found in the South who saw it as a scheme to perpetuate the advantage the North had over the developing world. The provisions surrounding TRIPs made illegal the trade in products containing any technology less than 20 years old, unless it was in line with the specifications of the current holder of the patent. Virtually all holders of intellectual property rights are situated in the North—only 0.16 percent of world patents are held by residents of the South. This fact essentially means that most (patented) technological innovations come from OECD countries, and their ability to withhold this technology—or to set their own price for it—will hamper the efforts of developing economies to grow. As one analyst put it, the WTO's regulations concerning TRIPs transformed the "owner of a technical process into a separate legal entity distinct not only from the laborer but also the factory or farm owner and the original inventor. They transform the ownership and control of technology into a marketable instrument of domination . . . set[ting] in concrete the principal market mechanism that impoverishes the Third World, namely the transfer of technological superprofit through trade."[6]

In an appeal against what was perceived as the hypocrisy of the North over "free trade," opponents of the TRIPs provisions also argued that the WTO's agenda was based on the reduction of trade barriers and that the rules surrounding intellectual property rights were actually a reversal of this, designed to protect the North from competition from the South. Indeed resistance from the South meant that there could be no agreement on a worldwide limit on the expiry of some intellectual property rights—patents for instance—although the essentially Northern-based pharmaceutical industry was conferred a five-year marketing monopoly on new products. Furthermore, states in the South have the ability to delay the complete compliance of the TRIPs agreement for up to 10 years.

### *Trade Related Investment Measures (TRIMs)*

This agreement lays down the rule that local content and trade balancing requirements are against GATT national treatment regulations. Six types of TRIMs are prohibited which are seen as attempts to direct or control foreign investment. For the South perhaps one of the most worrisome of these new rulings is on local content requirements and trade balancing requirements that compel investors to export as much as they import. This will be abolished.[7] Such new rules profoundly undermine the ability of developing countries to impose conditions on foreign investors. For sure, this prescription is in the interests of transnational corporations who will benefit from the "liberalization" of the investment procedure, but it is likely to see many small-scale domestic businesses in the South collapse in the face of the arrival of Northern mega corporations.

In essence, the WTO was founded as one of the main structures of global governance in an increasingly globalized international political economy, forming the third arm of what the G-77 chairman, Luis Fernando Jaramillo termed in a speech in New York in January 1994 "a New Institutional Trinity [whose] specific function [is] to control and dominate the economic relations that commit the developing world." This body was granted far-ranging disciplinary powers that saw its surveillance mission widened beyond that of GATT to encompass sectors previously governed by protectionist policies, such as textiles and agriculture, as well as what has already been referred to as "new" issues—regulation of investment measures, services, intellectual property rights and so on.

## UNCTAD's involvement

During the era when the GATT regime was at its height, developing countries were in a position where they could seek to neutralize the application of the liberalizing thrust of the agreements by banding together via multilateral bodies such as UNCTAD or the Non-aligned Movement. The first, as we have seen, was set up to promote the South's interests on the international trade front and thus aid development. Northern dominance of GATT was seen as problematic, though at the height of the NIEO era a number of developing countries engaged with the body during the Tokyo Round and in fact succeeded in obtaining the legalization of preferential tariff and nontariff treatment for the South in the form of the Generalized System of Preferences of 1971.[8] Essentially a two-tiered global system developed where the developing world, after hard and consistent lobbying, was exempted from the requirement to reciprocate in its trade with the North—a tacit recognition of the structural inequalities that the developing world suffered from and a reflection of the broadly *dependencista* ethos then current among those multilateral bodies such as UNCTAD dealing with the South's problems.

The reassertion of American-based domination over the Third World (a particular project of Reagan's) combined with the "lost decade" of chronic debt accumulation, in part worsened by the application of structural adjustment programs; and all within the overarching context of a global movement rightwards on economic policy at the expense of any redistributionist vision, profoundly altered the global balance of power. This was compounded by the switch in attention (what little there was) away from the South towards the East and the reconstruction of Eastern Europe according to liberal precepts, while the seemingly exponential growth of East Asia held out the temptation to Southern elites that export-based economies and international trade was the panacea to all their problems. Equally, as mentioned previously, there was a concerted attack against UNCTAD *as an organization* by the North. For instance, the Geneva-based Independent Commission on Global Governance "identified UNCTAD as one of the agencies that could be abolished in order to streamline the UN system. The commission's views apparently coincided with that of Karl Theodor Paschke, head of the newly created UN Office of Internal Oversight Services, who was quoted … as saying that UNCTAD had been made obsolete by the creation of the World Trade Organization (WTO)."[9]

South solidarity (understandably) largely evaporated in the face of such an onslaught and much of the developing world's behavior throughout the Uruguay Rounds (after being inextricably drawn into the process) was essentially rearguard attempts at warding off the more intolerable demands of the North. This had a deep impact upon

UNCTAD. In essence, much of the developing world went along with the provisions of the Uruguay Round out of fear of something worse. American willingness to tackle those administrations deemed out of step with prevailing "realities" and "common sense" was a major spur in this direction, particularly as American trade legislation—e.g. the 301 Trade Policy—provided for open and highly damaging discrimination against those states who supposedly had a weak intellectual property protection regime.

In short, like all other Rounds under GATT the Uruguay Round was marked by compromise, concessions and horse-trading. This was largely (though not exclusively) done among the major players—"the Quad" of the United States, Canada, the European Union and Japan—and the South, negotiating from a position of weakness and concerned at their continued marginalization, saw little option but to go along with the decisions of the predominant powers such as Europe and the United States. It is true that agricultural producers formed the Cairns Group to push for improved access to the protected markets of the OECD, but it is probably correct in suggesting that for many elites of the South, endorsement for the formation of the WTO centered around fear that failure to do so would stimulate a move by the North to concentrate on regional trading groups, i.e. NAFTA and the EU—a process which would only contribute to their further marginalization.

At the same time, many of the elites in the South had accepted much of the precepts of the neoliberalism project (see Chapter 4) and perhaps saw hope in the WTO as a vehicle by which the markets of the North could be truly opened up to competition from the developing world—a process which stood to benefit important fractions of the Southern-based elites (even if the reverse action threatened to impact negatively on the majority). This reflected the change in attitude towards GATT among much of the Southern elites. Formerly regarding the body as a "rich man's club," many had slowly accepted the "common sense" of neoliberalism and these elements from "the developing countries had become active and constructive participants in the ongoing GATT negotiations," seeking out the best deals they could for their local elites.[10]

Today, UNCTAD's posture towards the WTO is predicated on the position that liberal capitalism is the only viable strategy for nations to adopt and that integration into the world economy via an open liberal economy the key to promote development. As was detailed in earlier chapters, UNCTAD has arguably accepted the dominance of neoliberalism and the essential tenets and constraints of the ongoing order. In particular, the organization accepts that "investor friendly" policies are an ostensible precursor to investment capital flows and hence growth of the economies of the developing world. At the same time however, UNCTAD balances the desire to appear as reasonable as possible to the North (and also to fit with its members' wishes) with its commitment to redistributive goals inherited from its original founding purpose. One way the organization attempts to strike this balance—however contradictory this may actually be—is to adopt a reformist position. With regard to the WTO its stance is well within the remit of neoliberalism. Indeed, it has actually the potential to cause considerable embarrassment to the elites situated in the North. Essentially, at strategic moments and frequently in its research reports, UNCTAD turns the tables on the dominant powers in the global economy and highlights their hypocrisy vis-à-vis "free trade" and "liberalization."

This policy is based around the rhetoric of the "rules based" system that the WTO puts forward. Within such an international system, there are "obligations" that member states must abide by. At the same time, there are "rights" which a member state can expect and it is this flipside of the rules that UNCTAD often attempts to push in its engagement with the organization. For sure, UNCTAD accepts that the obligations stemming from membership of the WTO generally trump most concerns and broadly accedes to such prescriptions. Yet at the same time, UNCTAD pursues a policy to turn commitments within the WTO rules into concrete actualities and promote equal treatment for all in the name of development.

By putting forward such a position, UNCTAD has opened up space for maneuverability and indeed relevance for itself. Thus the organization has utilized declamatory statements of the WTO and the aspiration to craft a rules-based multilateral trading system and taken the supreme trade body at its word. This space is possible because unlike the IMF or the World Bank there is no inbuilt asymmetry of power between the various member states and so the global South has the (theoretical) ability to challenge major global players on their policies—something that could never happen in the North-dominated Bretton Woods bodies. This can be seen as an advance on the former (i.e. before the WTO regime) where decision-making was heavily in favor of the major players through their overbearing "trade weight."[11]

As a result of the more rules-based regulations, it has become possible for a state to force another to comply with the global trade rules as laid out by the WTO. This has been particularly directed against Washington, which has had to answer to the disciplinary body over its trading policies towards Argentina and Brazil as well as Massachusetts' unilateral ban on trade with Burma. The appeal to the WTO over the Helms-Burton Act is another example where the obligations of the North can be turned against them. However, at the same time, UNCTAD's selective engagement with the WTO and its periodic attempts to "delegitimize" certain actions by the major economic powers over their hypocritical selectivity in adhering to WTO regulations in various issue areas actually serves to legitimize the normative order that acts as a framework within which the WTO is situated and regulates. Indeed, UNCTAD's actions regarding the WTO seemingly demonstrate that the organization is a rules-based regime from which all can benefit and where even the South can confront and challenge the dominant developed powers. By doing so, it can be argued that UNCTAD usefully (for those who subscribe to the neoliberal order) undermines the argument that the WTO is serving the agenda purely of the privileged North for it is seen as critically engaging with and on occasion delegitimizing the dominant norms governing the international political economy. Yet, it does so without calling into question the fundamental structure that underpins these norms, nor does it interrogate the global order which keeps most of the South impoverished and disempowered—a concern of UNCTAD back in the 1960s and 1970s. Indeed, cynics might suggest that UNCTAD's engagement with the WTO and its ostensible delegitimization of specific practices by individual Northern nations actually obfuscates the broader and more central issues surrounding global inequality that have retreated into the background as the neoliberal consensus has achieved dominance.

## UNCTAD's overall relationship with the WTO

In recent times, the UNCTAD ministerial conferences have emphasized that research on trade and development issues is now one of the core businesses of the organization. Yet, this has become difficult as the WTO has assumed more and more power vis-à-vis trade rules, for if the WTO governs *global* trade, the place that UNCTAD fits within this schema in providing research on North-South relations is awkward. After all, how can UNCTAD maintain that its core activity is providing research analysis on trade-related matters when the practical side, i.e. actual consultation and dialogue on trade is under the remit of the WTO—and jealously guarded at that? And in fact the WTO is more and more assuming a research capacity on global trade issues that exposes UNCTAD as being—as its Northern critics might suggest—surplus to requirements. This is a conundrum that has developed as UNCTAD has ceded more and more ground to the WTO. In essence, it could be argued that UNCTAD has been backed into a corner whereby its relevancy has been effectively undermined as it has increasingly become a research and policy analysis forum.

Paradoxically, UNCTAD has been actively encouraging nations of the South to join the WTO—an organization which concomitantly undermines the exceptionality and arguably purpose of UNCTAD as the premier site for discussing trade and development. And as the WTO becomes larger and larger in terms of its membership, this problem is only going to grow and grow. Indeed, this problematique has been compounded by the exponential growth in the WTO's membership. Indeed, it is clear that very few states in the world are not—or will soon not—be members of the WTO. And of the 50 least developed countries on the UN list, 32 have become WTO members. It could be argued that for these remaining outsiders, UNCTAD *may* supply important research services and policy advice—although the IFIs, UN regional commissions and regional economic organizations turn out their own analysis and advice. Thus the value-added contribution of UNCTAD reports and services is under interrogation.

This in itself reflects the changes that have occurred within the global economy and in particular mirrors the dominant ideology that is an integral part of the ongoing order. As one analyst wrote, "the history of the developing countries in the world trading system reveals initial hostility to a regime that was controlled by advanced and industrialized countries. However it is obvious that the developing countries' attitudes [have changed]."[12] This attitudinal change has coincided with the rise to hegemony among the transnationalized elites of the neoliberal discourse, and the discrediting of dirigiste projects.

At the same time, it provides these selfsame elites with a "safety valve" by which they can protect (or attempt to) domestic industries against unfair foreign competition. With tariffs largely being taken away, antidumping measures can provide a degree of protection. Even if initiated cases are unsuccessful, by launching them an administration that is in the process of opening up its markets can present itself as having the welfare of domestic interests at heart and be seen to act in those interests—even if the reality is somewhat different and policy is being driven by more externally oriented elite fractions.

## Concluding remarks

In recent years UNCTAD has been pushing for a better working relationship with the WTO, as well as the IFIs. This wish to further increase the dialogue between the disciplinary institutions of neoliberalism and UNCTAD has been a feature of UNCTAD's broad position since the 1990s. This in part reflects a playing out of the increasing integration of the world's markets and the desire by local Southern-based elites to benefit from this process wherever possible. Combative posturing against the structural inequalities of the capitalist system, characteristic of the *dependencista* position, is seen to be of little use in facing up to globalization, particularly when much of the elites in the South subscribed to neoliberalism. Even those that do not fully accede to this "New World Order" are painfully aware of the ongoing marginalization that much of the South has been enduring. With the exception of Cuba and North Korea and possibly Venezuela, no state elites openly rejected the ideology of neoliberalism or the logic of the market.

This scenario currently marks the contemporary period, where neoliberalism is the hegemonic ideology vis-à-vis economic organization. As Mittelman and Pasha point out,

> Changes in global production and politics are reflected in the ideology of international organizations. They disseminate values and norms that contribute toward redesigning the global political economy. From the height of the Cold War to the more recent concerns of globalization, international institutions have absorbed the realities of global political economy and its contradictions. Imbued with neo-liberal doctrines, the current remedy for all ills is the market.[13]

Having said that, there has begun to emerge a nascent call within UNCTAD and other developmental multilateral sites for another NIEO. This is still very much at an embryonic stage as yet and needs further clarification, but it seems to the observer that there might be gathering momentum for what might be called a "post-hegemonic NIEO." This is in essence a synthesis of Modernization Theory-inspired precepts associated with neoliberal SAPs and what constitutes "good governance," but which equally asserts that the world order is currently heavily weighted in favor of the North and needs redressing, a position that links up (though its advocates would never admit it) with the insights of Dependency Theory.

UNCTAD has continued its broad trajectory as mentioned above but concern has increasingly been expressed that the historic bargain by the South to drop its confrontational posture in return for benefiting from globalization has been a largely one-sided affair. Certainly, how UNCTAD's developmental remit relates to the WTO has emerged as a site of concern for the South, particularly as the North opposes any reference to the implementation of specific WTO agreements, especially if developing countries suggest that the North is not honoring their responsibilities. Thus while the South has accepted a less-overtly hostile attitude to various international financial institutions and to the WTO, and indeed has actively facilitated forums where business can be involved in economic matters, the reform of various facets of the world economy has also been put onto the agenda.

In this milieu the WTO is seen as having strengthened the rules-based trading system, furthering liberalization and opening up opportunities for sustainable development and growth. Confrontation with the North has given way to "dialogue." Yet it is apparent that with the acceptance of the norms of trade liberalization and the implicit acceptance of the modernization project of the SAPs, goes a recognition of the uneven process of globalization. This has translated itself into a *partial* counter-hegemonic position that has called for a lessening of the worst aspects of this process.[14] Such impulses have informed the evolution of Africa's latest development plan, the New Economic Partnership for Africa's Development (NEPAD), although the fundamentally neoliberal (or at least post-Washington Consensus) underpinnings are quite clear.[15]

Though at a basic level elites in the South have embraced neoliberalism, with all its modernizing implications, they do seem aware of the negative downside and pressures that are concurrent with globalization. Thus leading elements within the South promote a reformist agenda aiming to "improve" the global system while promoting a more rules-based international regime. However, the viability of this call for a new world order remains open-ended.

Ultimately, UNCTAD sees itself as being complementary to the WTO: if the WTO's role is to remove barriers to global trade, UNCTAD's role is to assist developing countries in participating in such global trade, and especially in being able to take advantage of it. As a result, as has been mentioned previously, UNCTAD is now restructured into a division dealing with Globalization and Development Strategies, a division on International Trade, a division on Investment, Technology and Enterprise, a division on Services and Infrastructure, and a sub-division dedicated to the coordination of the work done for the least developed countries. Besides these divisions, UNCTAD has also reorganized into three Services for administrative support, i.e. Executive Direction and Management (including external relations), Administrative Services, and Intergovernmental Support Services.

Yet the future effectiveness of UNCTAD as an organization remains open to question. The Bangkok Declaration talked of how "UNCTAD must make a substantial contribution to the pursuit of development objectives" and how "it must also play an active role in consensus building around well-defined trade supporting and development issues."[16] But, as the head of the American delegation made clear, the North vigorously opposes any serious role for UNCTAD in international trade negotiations, as "an operational role for UNCTAD ... would involve a confusion of institutional roles and a diversion of limited resources for which UNCTAD is not the best-suited organization."[17]

Furthermore, at the Bangkok meeting, Carlos Fortin, UNCTAD's deputy secretary-general, openly admitted that when it comes to discussing global trade, UNCTAD has no negotiating authority; the WTO has that.[18] "It was a message that was repeated over the next two weeks at various forums. UNCTAD's role, said Secretary General Rubens Ricupero, was to provide good critical analysis of global economic developments, provide technical capacity training to developing countries entering the world trading system, and *build consensus* on key trade and development issues."[19] In other words, as an organization, UNCTAD has given up on trying to advance a better deal for the South in negotiations related to trade and has surrendered that right to the WTO. As Bello goes on to note, "the UNCTAD secretary general play[ed] a decisive leadership role in shaping a consensus on where the organization should be going [and] it was largely the dynamism of Raul Prebisch, UNCTAD's founder, that enabled UNCTAD in the late sixties to play a key role in securing global commodity agreements and preferential access to developed country markets of developing country exports."[20] In the face of antagonism from the North, the ascendancy of neoliberalism as the dominant ideology and the establishment of the WTO, such activism has been abandoned by the current Secretariat.

# Conclusion

As an organization, UNCTAD has had to navigate some extremely difficult problems and issues throughout its institutional history. Formed as a site for discussion on development issues, UNCTAD has had to face almost unremitting hostility from the developed world. The organization was, after all, formed because of dissatisfaction with the global trading order established after the Second World War at Bretton Woods. The BWIs, from the start, were controlled and dominated by the Northern countries. Consequently, as more and more new nations emerged in the post-colonial period, frustration with the ongoing order stimulated pressure for change. As the international trading system and GATT dealt primarily with the promotion of trade between the North, the United Nations (UN) system increasingly became sites where the South pushed for the codification of alternative norms of international trade and promotion of agreements that sought to stabilize the prices of primary commodities. As a result of UNCTAD discussions, agreements on a Generalized System of Preferences, providing for lower tariff rates for some exports from the South and on the creation of a Common Fund to help finance buffer stocks for commodity agreements were decided. This concession on the part of the North however was not nearly enough to satisfy the South, which pressed for a wide-ranging project that sought to redistribute wealth and begin to unravel the dependent relationships that held the South in a subordinate position vis-à-vis the North. Consequently, UNCTAD became an important site of contestation in the South's efforts to put forward the New International Economic Order (NIEO).

How and why UNCTAD then acceded to the dominant discourse of neoliberalism and how this must be contextualized within the constraints brought to bear upon UNCTAD is key to understanding the organization's current positions. The organization has largely moved away from inquisitions of the global trading regime per se to essentially problem-solving positions that seek to smooth out the international system. This is qualitatively different from the activist role that characterized UNCTAD in the 1960s/70s. Though this has been discussed in some detail, a combination of pressure, vested interests, threats and realism helped change UNCTAD into accepting—albeit reluctantly—that neoliberalism was the only "realistic" economic framework available. Yet, this has provoked a fundamental tension in UNCTAD's overall position, where on the one hand the organization accepts the fundamental normative world order (despite being an organization that ostensibly represents the South), and on the other pushes various reformist initiatives which seek to renegotiate the developing world's standing within this framework. Attempts to reconcile these two positions, of promoting "free" trade while at the same time demanding "fair" trade for example, mirror some fundamental contradictions evident in other forums, such as the WTO.

Yet, the policies and message contained within the neoliberal "package" can arguably only stand a chance of success within the South if the liberalization and free trade project is embarked upon with equal vigor in the developed world. Otherwise, liberalized industries in the developing world will be competing with protected manufacturers in the North—a scenario that can only impact negatively upon exports from the South. It is this sort of position that informs exporting countries of the developing world to accept the call for neoliberal restructuring at the WTO, but turn this rhetoric around and urge the developed world to engage in "real" free trade, rather than the "actually existing free trade" situation currently marking international commerce. This is basically UNCTAD's position today, although it should be pointed out that UNCTAD is not unique in this regard—such "pragmatic" policies have increasingly been transposed to specifically continental regional institutions in the developing world. In doing so, past "negative" rhetoric vis-à-vis dependency and neocolonialism have been quietly ditched.

This being said, UNCTAD should not be caricatured as being some sort of unquestioning tool of the West. Though at a basic level the organization and its Secretariat has embraced the convictions of neoliberalism, leading elements are cognizant of the negative downside and pressures that are concurrent with globalization. By engaging with the "objective" process of globalization rather than challenging it, it could be argued that UNCTAD as an organization sees such a tactical policy as the best way to ameliorate the contrary processes that impact negatively upon the global South. This in part springs from a particular understanding of the international political economy, which is seen as exerting forceful constraints on any alternative positions. Hence, the organization has opted for policy positions that exhibit a considerable amount of awareness to the forces that exact upon the global system, even if this results in an agenda that is at variance with the long-held positions of UNCTAD.

However, it must be said that such policies fail to interrogate the structural foundations of the international political economy while granting an important degree of legitimacy to this order. By engaging in essentially problem-solving behavior, UNCTAD today arguably contributes towards a reification of the global commonsense predicated upon the dominance of neoliberalism. Indeed, by agitating around basically technical issues, UNCTAD can be accused of helping to promote neoliberalism as the only viable framework and developmental agenda. Logically, the best choice that can be pursued in such a closed scenario is to advance a "tactical" engagement policy in order to maximize benefits.

Despite this, there are however some differences between UNCTAD's position and that of the BWIs. In general, the UN agencies maintain a stance that is essentially predicated upon broad issues of social justice and development, as opposed to the BWIs, who base their positions on perceived economic rationality and growth—the IMF more so than the World Bank. In short, the BWIs see the problems of the world as being centered around the inability of individuals and societies to adapt and/or adopt the market as the starting point for solutions to underdevelopment. The UN agencies in contrast generally take on board the issues associated with structural barriers to greater global equality and development. In this sense it can be argued that despite the apparent convergence of views, UNCTAD and the BWIs diverge in how they approach the globalized world political economy—the BWIs emphasize the prospects and breaks afforded developing countries by a globalized world while UNCTAD cautions against the risks and dangers. Thus the World Bank asserts that "global economic integration has supported poverty reduction and should not be reversed"[1] while UNCTAD warns against a simplistic embracing of globalization and its associated features. Indeed, in its report on *Economic Development in Africa*, UNCTAD warns that FDI carries costs as well as benefits for Africa and as a result urges that a more critical approach to evaluating the size, type, and impact of FDI in African countries is needed. Rather than the one-sided emphasis on attracting FDI, which is what the BWIs essentially advance, UNCTAD cautions for a more balanced and strategic approach.[2] It is certainly true that despite the convergence around basic policies, UNCTAD does remain more interventionist than the BWIs.

However, although UNCTAD still carries within its body the residue of the Dependency moment in the 1970s, it is apparent that objections raised by elite delegations from the South within UNCTAD at the global order are a pot-pourri of—often contradictory—agendas, ranging from the demand for global reform, to special treatment for Southern exporters, to equal treatment for the same. This is the same as at the WTO. Reforms being advocated by the leading nations within the G-77 are increasingly cast as sensible strategic choices. This mirrors the broader political debate about global governance.

Having said that, if UNCTAD is to remain a site of cutting edge and innovative work, its research studies must become more focused on the economic and social processes that would facilitate an increased dependence on the domestic market, thus granting space for the South to promote development with the pressures and constraints of a globalized world market. Yet, such a move would call into question the domestic arrangements of many countries of the South vis-à-vis their democratic credentials and commitments to the equitable distribution of resources. As Bello notes, "The indispensable and necessary links between growth, national sovereignty, and social reform must be placed at the centre of trade and development policy." However, as Bello further notes:

> The absence of serious attention to internal social reform owes itself to a simplistic North-South view of international economic relations. But equally important, UNCTAD has been too long a club of Southern governments and states that are uncomfortable at the examination of their internal political and economic arrangements.[3]

The implications for this are that UNCTAD needs to fundamentally rethink its existence as a multilateral body and its relationship both horizontally between states (i.e., North-South) and vertically *within* nations. While it is highly unlikely that UNCTAD will ever enjoy the heady days that characterized the 1960s and 1970s, the organization *does* have a role to play within the United Nations system and as its history has shown, the Secretariat has sought to navigate this future within an environment not necessarily of its choosing.

# Notes

## Foreword

1 See Rorden Wilkinson, *The WTO: Crisis and the Governance of Global Trade* (London: Routledge, 2006), chapter 3.
2 Theotonio dos Santos, "The Structure of Dependence," *American Economic Review* 60 (May 1970): 231–36.
3 UNCTAD, "Evaluation of UNCTAD's Trade-Related Technical Assistance and Capacity Building on Accession to the WTO," Trade and Development Board working party on the medium-term plan and the program budget forty-seventh session, UN document TD/B/WP/190, 21 July 2006.
4 See, for example, Thomas G. Weiss, *Multilateral Development Diplomacy in UNCTAD: The Lessons of Group Negotiations, 1964–1984* (London: Macmillan, 1986).
5 Ian Taylor, *China and Africa: Engagement and Compromise* (London: Routledge, 2006); *NEPAD: Towards Africa's Development or Another False Start* (Boulder, CO: Lynne Rienner, 2005); and *Stuck in Middle Gear: South Africa's Post-Apartheid Foreign Relations* (Westport, CT: Praeger, 2001).

## Introduction

1 Joseph Nye, "UNCTAD: Poor Man's Pressure Group," in *The Anatomy of Influence: Decision-making in International Organizations,* ed. Robert Cox and Harold Jacobson (New Haven, CT: Yale University Press, 1973), 334.
2 Ibid.
3 Robert S. Walters, "UNCTAD: Intervener Between Poor and Rich States," *Journal of World Trade Law* 7, no. 5 (1973): 527–54.
4 UNCTAD Proceedings of the United Nations Conference on Trade and Development, (I), Final Act and Report, E/CONF, 46/141 (I) (New York: United Nations, 1964).
5 Brian Hindley, "The UNCTAD Agreement on Preferences," *Journal of World Trade Law* 5, no. 6 (1971): 694–702.

## 1 Historical background

1 John White, "The New International Economic Order: What Is It?" *International Affairs* 54 (October 1978): 626–34.

2 Roeslan Abdulgani, *The Bandung Connection* (Jakarta: Gunung Agung, 1981); George McTurnan Kahin, *The Asian-African Conference* (Ithaca, NY, New York: Cornell University Press, 1956).
3 Robert A. Mortimer, *The Third World Coalition in International Politics* (Boulder, CO: Westview Press, 1984), 9.
4 Ibid.
5 Graham Evans and Jeffrey Newnham, *Dictionary of World Politics: A Reference Guide to Concepts, Ideas and Institutions* (Hemel Hempstead: Harvester Wheatsheaf, 1992).
6 See Boris C. Swerling, "Problems of International Commodity Stabilization," *American Economic Review* 53, no. 2 (1963): 65–74; Raymond F. Mikesell, "International Commodity Stabilization Schemes and the Export Problems of Developing Countries," *American Economic Review* 53, no. 2 (1963): 75–92.
7 UNCTAD, *The History of UNCTAD 1964–1984* (New York: United Nations, 1985), 10.
8 Marc Williams, *International Economic Organisations and the Third World* (London: Harvester Wheatsheaf, 1994), 183.
9 G.J. Butler, "Prebisch's Rationale for Protection," *Journal of Development Studies* 7, no. 3 (1971): 285–91.
10 Raul Prebisch, *Towards a New Trade Policy for Development* (New York: United Nations for UNCTAD, 1964), 6.
11 Ibid., 28.
12 M. June Flanders, "Prebisch on Protectionism: An Evaluation," *Economic Journal,* no. 294 (1964): 305–26.
13 Bernard D. Nossiter, *The Global Struggle for More* (New York: Harper and Row, 1987), 45.
14 UNCTAD, *The History of UNCTAD 1964–1984*, 34.
15 Richard N. Gardner, "The United Nations Conference on Trade and Development," *International Organization* 21 (September 1967): 685–704.
16 Hollis B. Chenery, "The Structuralist Approach to Development Policy," *The American Economic Review* LXV, no. 2 (1975): 310–16; Hans Singer, "Ideas and Policy: The Sources of UNCTAD," *IDS Bulletin* (July 1984): 14–17.
17 John H. Jackson, "The Puzzle of GATT: Legal Aspects of a Surprising Institution," *Journal of World Trade Law* 1, no. 2 (1967): 131–61.
18 Robert Ramsay, "UNCTAD's Failure: The Rich Get Richer," *International Organization* 38, no. 2 (1984): 388–9.
19 Harry G. Johnson, "A Strategy for UNCTAD," *Round Table,* no. 229 (1968): 7–13.
20 Samuel K.B. Asante, "The Role of the Organisation of African Unity in Promoting Peace, Development and Regional Security in Africa," in *Africa: Perspectives on Peace and Development,* ed. Emmanuel Hansen (London: Zed Books, 1987), 132.
21 Bernard D. Nossiter, *The Global Struggle for More* (New York: Harper and Row, 1987), 42–3.
22 Thierry de Montbrial, "For a New World Economic Order," *Foreign Affairs* 54, no. 1 (1975): 61–78.
23 Charles L. Robertson, "The Creation of UNCTAD," in *International Organization: World Politics,* ed. Robert Cox (London: Macmillan, 1969), 258.

24 Ivor Richard, "The United Nations and the New International Economic Order," *Millennium* 4, no. 1 (1975): 67–71.
25 *Dependencia* is a set of theories or worldview that are grounded on the hypothesis that external dependency characterizes the political economy of developing countries, facilitating exploitation. *Dependencia* theories argue that the dependency of colonies upon the metropoles was caused by the devastation of indigenous communities and economies and that the nature by which colonial territories were forcibly integrated into the global division of labor resonates in the contemporary era, perpetuating global inequality and exploitation.
26 Craig Murphy, *The Emergence of the NIEO Ideology* (Boulder, CO: Westview, 1984), 114.
27 Ervin Laszlo, Robert Baker, Elliot Eisenberg and Venkata Raman, *The Objectives of the New International Economic Order* (New York: Pergamon, 1979).
28 Gerry Helleiner, "Standing up to the World: The New Mood in the Less Developed Countries," *Development Dialogue,* no. 2 (1974): 12–18.
29 Enrico Augelli and Craig Murphy, *America's Quest for Supremacy and the Third World: A Gramscian Analysis* (London: Pinter Publishers, 1988).
30 Robert Lensink, *Structural Adjustment in Sub-Saharan Africa* (London: Longman, 1996).
31 World Bank, *Accelerated Development in Sub-Saharan Africa: An Agenda for Action* (Washington, DC: World Bank, 1981).
32 Martin Bronfenbrenner, "Predatory Poverty on the Offensive: The UNCTAD Record," Review Article, *Economic Development and Cultural Change* 24, no. 4 (1976): 831.
33 Ian M. Little, Richard N. Cooper, W. Max Corden, and Sarath Rajapatirana, *Boom, Crisis, and Adjustment: The Macroeconomic Experience of Developing Countries* (Oxford: Oxford University Press, 1994).
34 Kidane Mengisteab and Bernard I. Logan, *Beyond Economic Liberalization in Africa: Structural Adjustment and the Alternatives* (London: Zed Books, 1995).
35 Charles Harvey, ed., *Constraints on the Success of Structural Adjustment Programmes in Africa* (London: Macmillan, 1996).

## 2 UNCTAD's Secretariat structure

1 Charles Gore, "Global Interdependence and National Development Strategies," in *Beyond Conventional Wisdom in Development Policy: An Intellectual History of UNCTAD 1964–2004,* ed. Charles Gore and Shigehisa Kasahara (Geneva: United Nations, 2004), 46.
2 See Rubens Ricupero, "Nine Years at UNCTAD: A Personal Testimony," in *Beyond Conventional Wisdom in Development Policy: An Intellectual History of UNCTAD 1964–2004,* ed. Charles Gore and Shigehisa Kasahara (Geneva: United Nations), xiv.
3 Alexei Mojarav and Mehmet Arda, "Commodities," in *Beyond Conventional Wisdom in Development Policy: An Intellectual History of UNCTAD 1964–2004,* ed. Charles Gore and Shigehisa Kasahara (Geneva: United Nations, 2004), 61.
4 Shigehisa Kasahara, "Services in Development," in *Beyond Conventional Wisdom in Development Policy: An Intellectual History of UNCTAD 1964–2004,*

ed. Charles Gore and Shigehisa Kasahara (Geneva: United Nations, 2004), 120.

5 UNCTAD, *Services and the Development Process* (UNCTAD/ECDC/179) 1985.

6 Kasahara, "Services in Development," 121.

7 Murray Gibbs and Victor Ognivtsev, "International Trade," in *Beyond Conventional Wisdom in Development Policy: An Intellectual History of UNCTAD 1964–2004,* ed. Charles Gore and Shigehisa Kasahara (Geneva: United Nations, 2004), 7.

8 UNCTAD, *Trade in Services: Sectoral Issues* (New York: UNCTAD, 1989).

9 Gibbs and Ognivtsev, "International Trade," 8.

10 Kasahara, "Services in Development," 120.

11 UNCTAD, *Division on Investment, Technology and Enterprise Development (DITE) Activities Report 2005* (Geneva: United Nations, 2006), 10.

12 Torbjörn Fredriksson and Zbigniew Zimny, "Foreign Direct Investment and Transnational Corporations," in *Beyond Conventional Wisdom in Development Policy: An Intellectual History of UNCTAD 1964–2004,* ed. Charles Gore and Shigehisa Kasahara (Geneva: United Nations, 2004), 132.

13 For a more detailed discussion of TNCs, FDI and the UN system, and in particular how the UN has contributed to changing perceptions about the role of TNCs, see Tagi Sagafi-nejad, in collaboration with John Dunning, *The UN and Transnational Corporations, From Code to Compact* (Bloomington, IN: Indiana University Press, forthcoming).

14 UNCTAD, *Division on Investment, Technology and Enterprise Development (DITE*): Overview of Activities in 2005, www.unctad.org/en/docs/webite20061_en.pdf

15 Torbjörn Fredriksson and Zbigniew Zimny, "Foreign Direct Investment and Transnational Corporations," 127.

16 The *WIR* replaced the series of *Transnational Corporations in World Development*, which was published by the UNCTC.

17 UNCTAD, *Division on Investment, Technology and Enterprise Development (DITE*): Overview of Activities in 2005, 1.

18 See Assad Omer, Yehia Soubra and Victor Konde, "Technology," in *Beyond Conventional Wisdom in Development Policy: An Intellectual History of UNCTAD 1964–2004,* ed. Charles Gore and Shigehisa Kasahara (Geneva: United Nations, 2004), 82.

19 Ibid., 85.

20 Ibid., 86–7.

21 UNCTAD, *Division on Investment, Technology and Enterprise Development (DITE*): Overview of Activities in 2005, 2.

22 Awni Behnam and Peter Faust, "Shipping," in *Beyond Conventional Wisdom in Development Policy: An Intellectual History of UNCTAD 1964–2004,* ed. Charles Gore and Shigehisa Kasahara (Geneva: United Nations, 2004), 74.

23 For a detailed discussion of the meaning of the category of least developed countries (LDCs) and about the criteria which would be used to determine which countries could be classified as LDCs, see Thomas G. Weiss and Anthony Jennings, *More for the Least? Prospects for Poorest Countries in the Eighties* (Lexington, KY: Lexington Books, 1983), 1–29 and Lev

Komlev and Pierre Encontre, "Least Developed, Landlocked and Island Developing Countries," in *Beyond Conventional Wisdom in Development Policy: An Intellectual History of UNCTAD 1964–2004,* ed. Charles Gore and Shigehisa Kasahara (Geneva: United Nations, 2004), 104–5.

24 Ibid., 103, footnote 1.

25 For a detailed analysis of the Paris Conference, see Thomas G. Weiss and Anthony Jennings, *More for the Least? Prospects for the Poorest Countries in the Eighties* (Lexington: Lexington Books, 1983).

26 *Report of the Third United Nations Conference on the Least Developed Countries* (General Assembly document A/CONF.191/13), September 2001, para. 6.

27 Ibid., 105.

28 Ibid., 109–11.

29 Ibid., 109.

30 In 1984, ECLA became the Economic Commission for Latin America and the Caribbean (ECLAC).

31 See Thomas G. Weiss, *Multilateral Development Diplomacy in UNCTAD: The Lessons of Group Negotiations, 1964–1984* (Basingstoke: Palgrave, 1986).

**3 Research, analysis and major publications**

1 To access UNCTAD publications that are available electronically, go to www.unctad.org/publications.

2 Murray Gibbs and Victor Ognivtsev, "International Trade," in *Beyond Conventional Wisdom in Development Policy: An Intellectual History of UNCTAD 1964–2004,* ed. Charles Gore and Shigehisa Kasahara (Geneva: United Nations, 2004), 3.

3 Rubens Ricupero, "Nine Years at UNCTAD: A Personal Testimony," in *Beyond Conventional Wisdom in Development Policy: An Intellectual History of UNCTAD 1964–2004,* ed. Charles Gore and Shigehisa Kasahara (Geneva: United Nations, 2004), xii.

4 Torbjörn Fredriksson, "Forty Years of UNCTAD Research on FDI," *Transnational Corporations* 12, no. 3 (2003): 35.

5 *UNCTAD and Civil Society: Towards Our Common Goals* (UNCTAD document TD/382 /10/02/00) 2000, 5.

6 Ricupero, "Nine Years at UNCTAD: A Personal Testimony," xiv.

7 Gibbs and Ognivtsev, "International Trade," 15.

8 South Centre, *Reinventing UNCTAD* (Geneva: South Centre, 2006), 4.

9 *Implementation of the São Paulo Consensus—Report by the UNCTAD Secretariat to the 23rd Special Session of the Trade and Development Board* (UNCTAD document TD/B(S-XXIII)/2/Add.1), 26 April 2006.

10 For a comprehensive overview of UNCTAD's publications, see www.unctad.org/publications.

11 For a list of TDRs that are available electronically, see www.unctad.org/tdr.

12 UNCTAD, *Trade and Development Report 1996* (New York and Geneva: United Nations, 1996).

13 UNCTAD, *Trade and Development Report 1994* (New York and Geneva: United Nations, 1994).

14 UNCTAD, *Trade and Development Report 1997: Globalization, Distribution and Growth* (New York and Geneva: United Nations, 1997).

15 UNCTAD, *Trade and Development Report 2002: Developing Countries in World Trade* (New York and Geneva: United Nations, 2002).
16 UNCTAD, *Trade and Development Report 2005: New Features of Global Interdependence* (New York and Geneva: United Nations, 2005).
17 UNCTAD, *Trade and Development Report 2006: Global Partnership and National Policies for Development* (New York and Geneva: United Nations, 2006).
18 For a list of *WIR*s that are available electronically, see www.unctad.org/wir.
19 The first list of the world's top 100 TNCs was introduced in *WIR 1993*.
20 UNCTAD, *World Investment Report 1991: The Triad in Foreign Direct Investment* (New York and Geneva: United Nations, 1991).
21 UNCTAD, *World Investment Report 1993: Transnational Corporations and Integrated International Production* (New York and Geneva: United Nations, 1993).
22 Quoted in Fredriksson, "Forty Years of UNCTAD Research on FDI," 35.
23 UNCTAD, *World Investment Report 1999: FDI and the Challenge of Development* (New York and Geneva: United Nations, 1999).
24 UNCTAD, *World Investment Report 1998: Trends and Determinants* (New York and Geneva: United Nations, 1998).
25 UNCTAD, *World Investment Report 2000: Cross-border M&A and Development* (New York and Geneva: United Nations, 2000).
26 UNCTAD, *World Investment Report 2005: TNCs and the Internationalization of R&D* (New York and Geneva: United Nations, 2005).
27 UNCTAD, *World Investment Report 2001: Promoting Linkages* (New York and Geneva: United Nations, 2001).
28 UNCTAD, *World Investment Report 2002: Transnational Corporations and Export Competitiveness* (New York and Geneva: United Nations, 2002).
29 UNCTAD, *World Investment Report 2003: FDI Policies for Development: National and International Perspectives* (New York and Geneva: United Nations, 2003).
30 UNCTAD, *Division on Investment, Technology and Enterprise Development (DITE) Activities Report 2005* (Geneva: United Nations, 2006), 17.
31 *UNCTAD and Civil Society: Towards Our Common Goals. Note by the UNCTAD Secretariat* (UNCTAD document TD/382), 10 February 2000.
32 For a list of IPRs that are available electronically, see www.unctad.org/ipr.
33 For a list of LDCRs that are available electronically, see www.unctad.org/ldcr.
34 Stephen D. Younger, "Book Review: The Least Developed Countries Report 2002: Escaping the Poverty Trap," *Journal of African Economies* 12, no. 4 (2003): 672.
35 UNCTAD, *Least Developed Countries Report 2002: Escaping the Poverty Trap* (New York and Geneva: United Nations, 2002).
36 The PRSP approach was introduced in 1999 by the Bretton Woods Institutions following the dismal economic performance of the LDCs under the structural adjustment programs (SAPs).
37 UNCTAD, *Least Developed Countries Report 2000: Aid, Private Capital Flows and External Debt* (New York and Geneva: United Nations, 2000).
38 UNCTAD, *Least Developed Countries Report 2004: Linking International Trade with Poverty Reduction* (Geneva: United Nations, 2004).
39 UNCTAD, *Least Developed Countries Report 2006: Developing Productive Capacities* (Geneva: United Nations, 2006).

40 UNCTAD, *Least Developed Countries Report 1999: Marginalization, Productive Capacities and the LDCs* (Geneva: United Nations, 1999).
41 For a list of RMTs that are available electronically, see www.unctad.org/rmt.
42 UNCTAD, *Review of Maritime Transport 2005* (New York and Geneva: United Nations, 2005).
43 UNCTAD, *Review of Maritime Transport 2004* (New York and Geneva: United Nations, 2004).
44 UNCTAD, *Review of Maritime Transport 2003* (New York and Geneva: United Nations, 2003).
45 See www.unctad.org/statistics.
46 Ibid., 5.
47 Ibid., 5.
48 *Implementation of the São Paulo Consensus—Report by the UNCTAD Secretariat to the 23rd Special Session of the Trade and Development Board* (UNCTAD document TD/B(S-XXIII)/2/Add.1), 26 April 2006.
49 South Centre, *Reinventing UNCTAD,* 18–19.

**4 "Golden years," 1960s–1970s**

1 See Joseph Gusfield, "Tradition and Modernity," in *Social Change,* ed. Amitai Etzioni and Eva Etzioni-Halevy (New York: Basic Books, 1973), 333–41; and Richard F. Salisbury, *From Stone to Steel* (Cambridge: Cambridge University Press, 1962).
2 See Walter Rodney, *How Europe Underdeveloped Africa* (London: Bogle L'Ouverture Publications, 1972).
3 Geoffrey Kay, *Development and Underdevelopment: A Marxist Analysis* (London: Macmillan, 1975); Samir Amin, *Unequal Development* (New York: Monthly Review Press, 1976).
4 Andre G. Frank, *On Capitalist Underdevelopment* (Bombay: Oxford University Press, 1975).
5 Immanuel Wallerstein, *The Modern World System: Capitalist Agriculture and the Origins of the European World-Economy in the Sixteenth Century* (New York: Academic Press, 1974); Immanuel Wallerstein, *The Capitalist World Economy* (Cambridge: Cambridge University Press, 1979).
6 Fernando Henrique Cardoso and Enzo Faletto, *Dependency and Development in Latin America* (Berkeley, CA: University of California Press, 1979).
7 Kwame Nkrumah, *Neo-Colonialism: The Last Stage of Imperialism* (London: Nelson, 1965).
8 Andre G. Frank, *Capitalism and Underdevelopment in Latin America: Historical Studies of Chile and Brazil* (New York: Monthly Review Press, 1967).
9 Robert Cox and Harold Jacobson, *The Anatomy of Influence: Decision Making in International Organizations* (New Haven, CT: Yale University Press, 1973), 425.
10 Eric Helleiner, *States and the Re-emergence of Global Finance: From Bretton Woods to the 1990s* (Ithaca, NY: Cornell University Press, 1994).
11 Kees Van der Pijl, *The Making of an Atlantic Ruling Class* (London: Verso, 1984).
12 Samir Amin, *Delinking: Towards a Polycentric World* (London: Zed Books, 1985).

13 See for example, Raff Carmen, *Autonomous Development: Humanising the Landscape: An Excursion into Radical Thinking and Practice* (London: Zed Books, 1996); and Kidane Mengisteab, *Globalization and Autocentricity in Africa Development in the 21st Century* (Trenton: Africa World Press, 1996).
14 Robert L. Rothstein, *Global Bargaining: UNCTAD and the Quest for a New International Economic Order* (Princeton, NY: Princeton University Press, 1979).
15 Thomas G. Weiss, Tatiana Carayannis, Louis Emmerij and Richard Jolly, eds., *UN Voices: The Struggle for Development and Social Justice* (Bloomington, IN: Indiana University Press, 2005), 194.
16 Jahangir Amuzegar, "The North-South Dialogue: From Conflict to Compromise," *Foreign Affairs* 54, no. 3 (1976): 56–65.
17 Beverly J. Silver and Giovanni Arrighi, "Workers North and South," in *Socialist Register 2001: Working Classes, Global Realities*, ed. L. Panitch and C. Leys (London: Merlin Press, 2000), 66–7.
18 Kelly Lee, "A Neo-Gramscian Approach to International Organization: An Expanded Analysis of Current Reforms to UN Development Activities," in *Boundaries in Question: New Directions in International Relations,* ed. Andrew Linklater and John Macmillan (Basingstoke: Macmillan, 1995), 156.
19 Sidney Wells, "The Developing Countries, GATT and UNCTAD," *International Affairs* 45, no. 1 (1969): 64–79.
20 Weiss, Carayannis, Emmerij and Jolly, eds., *UN Voices: The Struggle for Development and Social Justice*, 194.
21 Rosemary Righter, *Utopia Lost: The United Nations and World Order* (New York: Twentieth Century Fund Press, 1995), 27.
22 Craig Murphy, *The Emergence of the NIEO Ideology* (Boulder, CO: Westview, 1984), 114.
23 Gamani Corea, "North-South Dialogue at the United Nations: UNCTAD and the New International Economic Order," *International Affairs* 53, no. 2 (1977): 177–87.
24 Robert A. Mortimer, *The Third World Coalition in International Politics* (Boulder, CO: Westview Press, 1984), 52.
25 Dietrich Kebschull, "Trade and Development: UNCTAD III—One More Disappointment," *Intereconomics* 7 (September 1972): 72–7.
26 Colin Kirkpatrick, "UNCTAD V: Issues and Prospects," *Journal of World Trade Law* 13, no. 3 (1979): 409–36.
27 Harry Shutt, *The Trouble with Capitalism: An Enquiry into the Causes of Global Economic Failure* (London: Zed Books, 1998), 28.
28 Robert Biel, *The New Imperialism: Crisis and Contradictions in North/South Relations* (London: Zed Books, 2000), 126.
29 Jagdish N. Bhagwati, "Rethinking Global Negotiation," in *Power, Passions and Purpose: Prospects for North-South Negotiation,* ed. Jagdish N. Bhagwati and John Gerard Ruggie (Cambridge, MA: MIT Press, 1984), 25.
30 Charles A. Jones, *The North-South Dialogue: A Brief History* (New York: St Martin's Press, 1983).
31 Geoffrey Goodwin and James Mayall, "The Political Dimensions of the UNCTAD Integrated Commodity Scheme," *Millennium* 6, no. 2 (1977): 146–61.

32 Keld Laursen, "The Integrated Programme for Commodities," *World Development* 6, no. 4 (1978): 437–45.
33 Jones, *The North-South Dialogue: A Brief History*, 36.
34 Marc Williams, *International Organizations and the Third World* (Hemel Hempstead: Harvester Wheatsheaf, 1994), 194.
35 Enrico Augelli and Craig Murphy, *America's Quest for Supremacy and the Third World: A Gramscian Analysis* (London: Pinter Publishers, 1988), 150–1.
36 Quoted by Fred Halliday, "The Maturing of the Non-Aligned: Perspectives from New Delhi," *Third World Affairs, 1985* (London: Third World Foundation for Social and Economic Studies, 1985), 48.
37 Louis W. Pauly, *Who Elected the Bankers? Surveillance and Control in the World Economy* (Ithaca, NY: Cornell University Press, 1997), 32.
38 South Commission, *The Challenge to the South: The Report of the South Commission* (Oxford: Oxford University Press, 1990).
39 Post-Fordism is the name given to the industrial model of production born in the 1970s and is characterized by customer-centered service and a high degree of flexibility.
40 Riccardo Faini and Enzo Grilli, eds., *Multilateralism and Regionalism after the Uruguay Round* (Basingstoke: Macmillan, 1997), xiii.
41 Robert W. Cox, *Approaches to World Order* (Cambridge: Cambridge University Press, 1996), 206.
42 Weiss, Carayannis, Emmerij and Jolly, eds., *UN Voices: The Struggle for Development and Social Justice*, 198.

**5 UNCTAD's crisis, retreat and reinvention, 1980s onwards**

1 See John Williamson, "Democracy and the 'Washington Consensus,'" *World Development* 21, no. 8 (1993): 1329–36.
2 Enrico Augelli and Craig Murphy, *America's Quest for Supremacy and the Third World: A Gramscian Analysis* (London: Pinter Publishers, 1988), 189.
3 Margaret Thatcher, *The Downing Street Years* (London: Harper and Collins, 1993), 170.
4 UNCTAD, *Securing Growth and Development: A Guide to UNCTAD* (Geneva: UNCTAD, 1994), 3.
5 Walden Bello, "UNCTAD X: An Opportunity Lost," *Focus on Trade*, no. 46 (February 2000): 55.
6 Walden Bello, *Brave New Third World: Strategies for Survival in the Global Economy* (London: Earthscan, 1990), 45.
7 J. J. G. Syatauw, "The Non-Aligned Movement at the Crossroads: The Jakarta Summit Adapting to the Post-Cold War Era," *Asian Yearbook of International Affairs* 3 (1993): 129.
8 Nana S. Sutresna, "Speech of H.E. Mr. Nana S. Sutresna at a Conference on 'South Africa and the Non-Aligned Movement' in Johannesburg on 10 June 1998," *Indonesia in Perspective* 9 (July 1998): 4.
9 Javed Ansari, *The Political Economy of International Economic Organization* (Brighton: Wheatsheaf Books, 1986), 274.
10 Craig Murphy, "The United Nations' Capacity to Promote Sustainable Development: The Lessons of a Year That 'Eludes All Facile Judgement,'" in *The State of the United Nations, 1992* (Providence, RI: Academic Council of the United Nations System, 1992), 270.

11 Kathryn C. Lavelle, "Ideas within a Context of Power: The African Group in an Evolving UNCTAD," *Journal of Modern African Studies* 39, no. 1 (2001): 38.
12 See, for instance, Gamani Corea, "North-South Issues: The UNCTAD Perspective," *Studia Diplomatica* 36, no. 1 (1983): 3–14.
13 Lavelle, "Ideas Within a Context of Power," 38.
14 Ibid., 39.
15 Stanley J. Michalak, *UNCTAD: Testing the Reagan Commitment to Third World Growth*, Heritage Foundation Backgrounder #530, 26 August 1985.
16 Thomas G. Weiss, "UNCTAD: What Next?" *Journal of World Trade Law* 19, no. 3 (1985): 251–68.
17 Michalak, *UNCTAD: Testing the Reagan Commitment to Third World Growth*, 2.
18 Quoted in Thomas G. Weiss, Tatiana Carayannis, Louis Emmerij and Richard Jolly, eds., *UN Voices: The Struggle for Development and Social Justice* (Bloomington, IN: Indiana University Press, 2005), 346.
19 Lavelle, "Ideas Within a Context of Power," 40.
20 A. F. Ewing, "The Assault on Development Economics: Consequences for Intergovernmental Co-operation," *Journal of World Trade Law* 18, no. 3 (1984): 189–205.
21 Carlston B. Boucher and Wolfgang E. Siebeck, "UNCTAD VII: New Spirit in North-South Relations: A Report on the Seventh United Nations Conference on Trade and Development," *Finance and Development* 24, no. 4 (December 1987): 14–16.
22 Marc Williams, "UNCTAD and International Economic Reform: A Note on Organizational Characteristics and the Political Process," in *Global Issues in the United Nations,* ed. P. Taylor and J. Groom (New York: St. Martins Press, 1989), 273–81.
23 Matthias Finger and Bérangère Ruchat, *The Transformation of International Public Organizations: The Case of UNCTAD*, Working Paper of IDHEAP 14/2000 (Lausanne: Institut de Hautes Etudes en Administration Publique, 2000).
24 John Ravenhill, "The North-South Balance of Power," *International Affairs* 66, no. 4 (1990): 731–48.
25 Lavelle, "Ideas within a Context of Power," 40.
26 Ron Sanders, "An Assessment of UNCTAD's Effectiveness as an Instrument to Promote the Interests of the Third World," *Round Table,* no. 311 (July 1989): 273–82.
27 UNCTAD, "A New Partnership for Development: The Cartagena Committment, Proceedings of the Report and Annexes," (United Nations Publication, Sales No. E.93 11.D.5), part one.
28 Craig Murphy, "The United Nations' Capacity to Promote Sustainable Development: The Lessons of a Year That 'Eludes All Facile Judgement,'" in *The State of the United Nations, 1992* (Providence, RI: Academic Council of the United Nations System, 1992), 63–4.
29 "The Spirit of Cartagena," 1992.
30 Walden Bello, "UNCTAD X: An Opportunity Lost," 55.
31 Berend Diekmann, "Is There a New Reforming Spirit at International Organizations? The Example of UNCTAD I," *Intereconomics* 51, no. 5 (1996): 222–3.

32 Ankie Hoogvelt, *Globalization and the Post-colonial World: The New Political Economy of Development* (London: Macmillan, 1997), 137.
33 Marc Williams, *International Organisations and the Third World* (Hemel Hempstead: Harvester Wheatsheaf, 1994), 179.
34 Rubens Ricupero, "UNCTAD: Enfant Terrible Hopes for Rebirth," *World Today* 52, no. 4 (April 1996): 106–7.
35 Marie-Claude Smouts, "International Organizations and Inequality Among States," *International Social Science Journal*, no. 144 (June 1995): 239.
36 Xavier Carim, *South Africa and UNCTAD IX: New Beginnings?* (Pretoria: Institute of Strategic Studies), Occasional paper no. 7, August 1996, 3.
37 Foreign and Commonwealth Office, *Background Brief: United Nations Conference on Trade and Development: UNCTAD IX* (London: FCO), no date.
38 For details and final resolutions at the Conference, see UNCTAD, *UNCTAD IX Midrand Declaration, 1995, South Africa*, www.sunsite. scu.eun.eg/untpdc/library/te/unctadix/u9midra.htm.
39 Ibid.
40 Department of Foreign Affairs, *Preparing for WTO Multilateral Trade Negotiations in 2000: Towards a South African Framework* (Pretoria: DFA, 1999), 8.
41 Carim, *South Africa and UNCTAD IX*, 5.
42 Interview with John Davies, Director, International Development and Economic Affairs, Department of Foreign Affairs, Pretoria, 8 July 1999.
43 Ibid.
44 Carim, *South Africa and UNCTAD IX*, 5.
45 Interview with Henry Raubenheimer, Deputy Director, Development and Finance, Department of Foreign Affairs, Pretoria, 21 July 1999.
46 Teteh Hormeku, "NGOs Critical of UNCTAD's Investment and Pro-Business Approach," *Third World Economics*, no. 187/188 (16 June–15 July 1998): 1.
47 Ibid. 2.
48 Interview with John Davies, Director, International Development and Economic Affairs, Department of Foreign Affairs, Pretoria, 8 July 1999.
49 Hormeku "NGOs Critical of UNCTAD's Investment and Pro-Business Approach," 6.
50 Diekmann, "Is There a New Reforming Spirit at International Organizations?" 226.
51 Quoted in Tim Wall, "Trade Climate Warms at UNCTAD X" *Africa Recovery* 14, no. 1 (2000): 4.
52 "Bangkok Declaration: Global Dialogue and Dynamic Engagement" (2000) Bangkok, 12–19 February, www.mofa.go.jp/policy/un/unctad/dec0002.html.
53 "UNCTAD X—Plan of Action," www.mofa.go.jp/policy/un/unctad/plan0002.html.
54 Martin Khor, "UNCTAD XI Ends in a Rather Good Spirit," Third World Network *Info Service on WTO Issues*, 22 June 2004.
55 Amrita Narlikar, *International Trade and Developing Countries: Bargaining Coalitions in the GATT and WTO* (London: Routledge, 2003).
56 The following is drawn in part from Ian Taylor, "The Periphery Strikes Back? The G-20 at the WTO," in *The WTO after Hong Kong: Progress in,*

*and Prospects for, the Doha Development Agenda,* ed. D. Lee and R. Wilkinson (London: Routledge, forthcoming).

57 Quoted in "Brazil, SA and India May Form Trade Bloc," *The Star* (Johannesburg), 29 January 2004.

58 South Bulletin, "G-20: A Powerful Tool for Convergence in Negotiations," 15 November 2003.

59 World Vision, "Cancun Collapse: Developing Countries Stand Firm, But Future Uncertain," 16 September 2003.

60 Ian Taylor, "The 'All-weather Friend'? Sino-African Interaction in the Twenty-first Century" in *Africa in International Politics: External Involvement on the Continent*, ed. Ian Taylor and Paul Williams (London: Routledge, 2004), 83–101.

61 See Chris Alden and Marco Antonio Vieira, "The New Diplomacy of the South: South Africa, Brazil, India and Trilateralism," *Third World Quarterly* 26, no. 7 (2005): 1077–95.

62 Hugo Ruiz-Diaz, "G-20: The South Fights for the South," *Le Monde Diplomatique* (September 2005): 12–13.

63 Simon Barber "Mbeki Bears Weight of Developing Countries, *Business Day*, 29 May 2000.

64 Mario Osava, "G-20 Might Just Add up for the WTO," *Inter Press Service*, 11 October 2003.

65 Enrinco Augelli and Craig Murphy, *America's Quest for Supremacy and the Third World: A Gramscian Analysis* (London: Pinter Publishers, 1988).

66 Ruiz-Diaz, "G-20: The South Fights for the South," 13.

67 Walden Bello "Washington's Vendetta," www.geocities.com/ericsquire/articles/ftaa/frontlin031025.htm.

68 Matt Eagleton-Pierce, "Doing the Canc?," *Oxford Student*, 2 October 2003.

**6 The multilateral trading system and the future: Where does UNCTAD fit into the WTO?**

1 See Bernard Hoekman and Michael Kostecki, *The Political Economy of the World Trading System: From GATT to WTO* (Oxford: Oxford University Press, 1995).

2 Ibid., 8.

3 Allan Freeman, "Fixing Up the World? GATT and the World Trade Organization," *Links*, no. 10 (March–July 1998): 82.

4 Shalendra D. Sharma, "The World Trade Organization and Implications for Developing Countries," *SAIS Review* 17, no. 2 (Summer–Fall 1997): 66.

5 Myriam van der Stichele, "World Trade: Free for Whom, Fair for Whom?" in *Challenges to the United Nations: Building a Safer World,* ed. Erskine Childers (New York: St. Martin's Press, 1995), 5.

6 Freeman, "Fixing Up the World?" 82.

7 Sharma, "The World Trade Organization," 67.

8 A formal scheme of exemption from the more general rules of the then GATT, now WTO.

9 Walden Bello, "UNCTAD X: An Opportunity Lost," *Focus on Trade*, no. 46 (February 2000): 55.

10 Michael Hart "The WTO and the Political Economy of Globalization," *Journal of World Trade* 31, no. 5 (October 1997): 76.
11 Chakravarthi Raghavan, *Recolonization: GATT, the Uruguay Round and the Third World* (London: Zed Books, 1990), 64.
12 Kofi Oteng Kufour, "The Developing Countries and the Shaping of GATT/WTO Antidumping Law," *Journal of World Trade* 32, no. 6 (1998): 194.
13 James H. Mittelman and Mustapha Kamal Pasha, *Out From Underdevelopment Revisited: Changing Global Structures and the Remaking of World Order* (Basingstoke: Macmillan, 1997), 53.
14 See Thandika Mkandawire and Charles C. Soludo, *Our Continent, Our Future: African Perspectives on Structural Adjustment* (Trenton: Africa World Press, 1999).
15 See Ian Taylor, *NEPAD: Towards Africa's Development or Another False Start?* (Boulder, CO: Lynne Rienner, 2005).
16 "Bangkok Declaration: Global Dialogue and Dynamic Engagement," Bangkok, 12–19 February 2000, www.mofa.go.jp/policy/un/unctad/dec0002.html.
17 Tim Wall, "Trade Climate Warms at UNCTAD X," *Africa Recovery* 14, no. 1 (2000).
18 Bello, "UNCTAD X: An Opportunity Lost," 2.
19 Ibid., 2.
20 Ibid., 3.

**7 Conclusion**

1 World Bank, *Globalization, Growth and Poverty: Building an Inclusive World Economy* (Washington: Oxford University Press, 2001), xi.
2 UNCTAD, *Economic Development in Africa: Rethinking the Role of Foreign Direct Investment* (Geneva: UNCTAD, 2005).
3 Walden Bello, "Building an Iron Cage: The Bretton Woods Institutions, the WTO, and the South," in *Views from the South: The Effects of Globalization and the WTO on the Third World,* ed. Sarah Anderson (New York: International Forum on Globalization, 2000), 1–34.

# Select bibliography


Enrico Augelli and Craig Murphy, *America's Quest for Supremacy and the Third World: A Gramscian Analysis* (London: Pinter Publishers, 1988). This book provides an innovative theoretical framework for understanding how and why neoliberalism became ascendant in the developing world, connected to American foreign policy interests.

Matthias Finger and Bérangère Ruchat, *The Transformation of International Public Organizations: The Case of UNCTAD* Working Paper de l'IDHEAP 14/2000 (Lausanne: Institut de Hautes Etudes en Administration Publique, 2000). This work provides an overview of how UNCTAD's policies and structures have changed.

Charles A. Jones, *The North-South Dialogue: A Brief History* (New York: St Martin's Press, 1983). This volume argues that too much rhetoric by UNCTAD may have damaged the organization's potential and that North-South "dialogue" is not as important as structural reform in the South and the liberalization of Northern trading regimes as a means of promoting economic development.

Stanley J. Michalak, *UNCTAD: Testing the Reagan Commitment to Third World Growth* Heritage Foundation Backgrounder #530, 26 August 1985. This work provides a flavor of the deep-seated hostility towards UNCTAD by neoliberals and conservatives. From a leading conservative and influential think-tank in Washington D.C.

Robert A. Mortimer, *The Third World Coalition in International Politics* (Boulder, CO: Westview Press, 1984). This book discusses the strengths and weaknesses of coalition forming by the developing world—such as the G-77—in global politics.

Craig Murphy, *The Emergence of the NIEO Ideology* (Boulder, CO: Westview, 1984). This book explains how and why NIEO proposals shifted and changed over time.

Robert L. Rothstein, *Global Bargaining: UNCTAD and the Quest for a New International Economic Order* (Princeton, PA: Princeton University Press, 1979). This book traces the origins and formation of UNCTAD and its role in promoting the NIEO.

UNCTAD, "The Spirit of Cartagena," declaration adopted by UNCTAD VIII, Cartagena de Indias, Colombia, 8–25 February 1992. Captures the new agenda and sense of "realism" that UNCTAD adopted as the 1990s began.

Thomas G. Weiss, Tatiana Carayannis, Louis Emmerij and Richard Jolly, eds., *UN Voices: The Struggle for Development and Social Justice* (Bloomington: Indiana University Press, 2005). This book comprises information drawn from interviews with 73 individuals who spent much of their lives in the United Nations system. The volume contains very interesting anecdotes and information about the thinking towards UNCTAD from inside and outside of the UN system, including interviews with several key members of the UNCTAD Secretariat.

Thomas G. Weiss, *Multilateral Development Diplomacy in UNCTAD: The Lessons of Group Negotiations, 1964–1984* (London: Macmillan, 1986). This volume provides an analysis from the inside of the heyday of North-South negotiations, especially the G-77 within UNCTAD gatherings.

Marc Williams, *International Organisations and the Third World* (Hemel Hempstead: Harvester Wheatsheaf, 1994). This book provides a useful overview of how multilateral bodies have engaged with the developing world over time.

# Index

For Product Safety Concerns and Information please contact our EU
representative GPSR@taylorandfrancis.com
Taylor & Francis Verlag GmbH, Kaufingerstraße 24, 80331 München, Germany

www.ingramcontent.com/pod-product-compliance
Ingram Content Group UK Ltd.
Pitfield, Milton Keynes, MK11 3LW, UK
UKHW022344190926
475702UK00015B/2092

* 9 7 8 0 4 1 5 3 7 0 1 9 6 *